From Oven Lane to Sun Prairie:
In Search of Irish America

Eamonn Wall

From Oven Lane to Sun Prairie:
In Search of Irish America

ARLEN
HOUSE

*From Oven Lane to Sun Prairie:
In Search of Irish America*

is published in 2019 by
ARLEN HOUSE
42 Grange Abbey Road
Baldoyle
Dublin 13
Ireland
Phone: +353 86 8360236
Email: arlenhouse@gmail.com

978–1–85132–209–1, paperback

International distribution by
SYRACUSE UNIVERSITY PRESS
621 Skytop Road, Suite 110
Syracuse, New York
USA 13244–5290
Phone: 315–443–5534/Fax: 315–443–5545
Email: supress@syr.edu
www.syracuseuniversitypress.syr.edu

© Eamonn Wall, 2019

The moral right of the author has been asserted

Typesetting by Arlen House

Cover Artwork: 'October Snow'
by Viva Kathleen Momaday
24" x 18" • oil on wood panel
reproduced courtesy of the artist
www.vivamomadayart.com

Contents

9   *Introduction & Acknowledgements*

19   The Truth about Himself:
     Derek Mahon in New York

67   Jean Valentine in Ireland

91   Irish American Fables of Resistance

109 Return to Finland:
     Robert Creeley, Continental Drift

125 The Habit of Land:
     Eavan Boland's Irish American Voice

147 Rory Gallagher's Blues

167 The Use of Memory:
     Michael Coady's *All Souls*

187 In Abiquiu:
     In Search of Georgia O'Keeffe

204 *About the Author*

205 *Index*

In Memory of Philip Casey
1950–2018

INTRODUCTION AND ACKNOWLEDGEMENTS

Like many of the Irish who immigrated to the USA during the 1980s I arrived with only limited knowledge of Irish America. The New Irish of that era, as our generation was called, came here seeking the novel and the electric to replace the familiarity of Irish ways and tired ideologies. Of course, we were also looking for employment – legal or not – and we professed no desire to be more Irish in America than we had been in Ireland. Perhaps in America, unconstrained by the carefully-imagined futures invented for us, we might develop new wings. I am sure it is provable that many of our generation succeeded dramatically while others flamed out spectacularly. For most of us, a settling-in period was followed by the immigrant imperative of getting-on-with-it in America. Today, nearly four decades on, America is every bit as captivating to me as it was when I first arrived.

Growing up County Wexford in the 1950s and 1960s I had only rarely met Americans. Just as Wexford people did not seem to travel to America much, so too did American visitors tend to bypass our county while on visits to the Old Country. Through childhood America was a more distant place than it is today. Then, as now, America was an idea with a singular energy driving it. Once, I remember a priest coming to visit my father who regaled us with an account of a recent visit he had made to 'Windows on the World' in the World Trade Center. In rapt attention we listened, gathered at his feet, at his otherworldly fable. Today, Wexford people will fly to America for a weekend of shopping while American visitors will hardly be granted a passing glance as their voices herald departure from our county museum. A parent living in New York in the 1980s, I would bring my children to the World Trade Center to play on summer days of poor air quality.

I can only remember a single childhood conversation with an American and that occurred when relatives of my mother's family from New Jersey called to our house. I heard later that my father had not approved of these visitors because they had criticised the Kennedys who, like us, belonged to Wexford. One of my father's cousins had served as a priest in Texas; however, being an Irish priest in Texas hardly counted as being American to my narrow way of thinking at the time. American television programmes became available in rural Ireland in the 1960s and this fare supplemented the cowboy films that excited us so much on the screen at Enniscorthy's Astor Cinema. As far as the primary school curriculum was concerned America was largely excluded. I knew that books on America were available in the local library; however, for many years I did not enter those premises fearing the wrath of Mrs Doyle, the librarian, and my fate as the borrower of a lost book.

Living in Dublin as a college student I would meet Americans. Our college curriculum was light on American literature. Though in my spare time I read American books, books about America, listened to American music and enjoyed American films, it never crossed my mind that I would leave Ireland to live there. I have been living in the

US since 1982, a period of thirty-seven years. My original plan – though this is probably too grandiose a term to use – was to go to live in Italy for a few years, become fluent in Italian as well as learn how to live in a foreign country, and then return to Ireland. When the teaching position I was promised in Italy fell through, James Liddy recommended me for a student/teaching position at the University of Wisconsin-Milwaukee. On one level my knowledge of American culture prepared me for America; however it in no way schooled me to live here as an immigrant. Each day I work to make up this deficit. It is likely that I understand America better now and Ireland not as well as I used to.

When I finally settled into my American life I grew interested in ethnic American writing, including books written by and about Irish America. In this respect I was fortunate to be guided by an inspiring teacher at the CUNY Graduate Center: Morris Dickstein opened the door to this new territory. Bernard Malamud's *The Magic Barrel*, a collection of short stories about the lives and loves of Jewish Americans, captured me and drove me on to explore the fiction, poetry, drama and prose written by Irish Americans. I am also indebted to the writers and scholars who have pushed the boundaries of Irish American scholarship: Charles Fanning, Daniel Tobin and Rebecca Solnit have been my guiding lights for this project. Also the works of James Silas Rogers, Janet Nolan, Jack Morgan, Maureen Murphy, Sally Barr Ebest, Ron Ebest, Laurence Welsh and others have helped me understand the field at a greater depth. For the past six years, I have been honoured to serve as a board member of Irish American Writers & Artists, an organisation dedicated to keeping Irish American cultural expression alive. My thanks to my fellow board members and special thanks to Mary Pat Kelly, current president of IAW&A, and past-president Larry Kirwan.

Though I had resisted it for years, the day I walked my eldest child to school for the first time was the day I became an Irish American. It was PS 98 in Inwood, New York. From then on, I would be identified to others as being Irish, meaning Irish American. Until that moment, I had lived in New York as an émigré, as one who lived in the US though was not of it. But as a parent who brought his son to school each morning and collected him every afternoon, I was absorbed into a larger world, like one fish happily caught in a giant American monofilament net. But, then and now, I feel a deep sense of belonging to a vibrant community of all immigrants in the US – we have arrived from every corner of the earth.

The writers, artists and musicians that I write about in this book are women and men defined by their complex attachments to place and places. In her Irish travelogue, Rebecca Solnit writes that:

> we are often in two places at once. In fact, we are usually in at least two places, and occasionally the contrast is evident. I always seem to be trailing through three or four at once ...[1]

My objective here is to explore the work of artists who belong to Ireland and America in various ways and at multiple levels, to reveal how what they have written, painted and performed resists simple binary notions of belonging. Of course, they belong first to their art – more than to any country – and to their bodies and psyches. This group that I have gathered is diverse and eclectic rather than canonical, but helpful when one seeks to complicate engagement to place. Binaries, such as Irish American, are broken down and, at least in part, revised or replaced by interdependence and exchange between Ireland and America. Often, like pieces of music, songs and poems, artists move back and forth between the US and Ireland, and with each movement artforms are subtly altered: in Rory Gallagher's reverent blues, for example, the music of the Mississippi Delta is reshaped by his Irish background.

All of these artists under consideration, and the chapters that comprise this study, are underlined by movement: physical, emotional, imaginative and psychological. Ireland maps America and America Ireland. Irish American artistic production today is, to borrow Neil Campbell's phrase, 'a traveling or mobile discourse' with artists as often between places as on the ground at home, and defined by travel rather than by 'dwelling'.[2]

Though artists may not reside for long in one or more Irish or American locations, they manage to establish deep connections to where they have found themselves – Derek Mahon in New York, Eavan Boland in Iowa City, Jean Valentine in County Sligo, Michael Coady in Philadelphia – that reshape their work. And all of this is defined by movement rather than by dwelling. Though this is largely a work of traditional scholarship, my approach has also been framed by narrative scholarship, a more hybrid way of working in this field, and one that can accommodate, when it is useful, a more personal discourse. It is study of movement written by a mobile immigrant. In this regard, I have been guided by the genre-bending works of Eavan Boland, Tim Robinson and Elizabeth Cook-Lynn.

Many of the chapters in this book were originally written as conference papers for American Conference for Irish Studies international and regional conferences. I am grateful to friends and colleagues in ACIS for their feedback, friendship and support over the years: Daniel Tobin, Christine Casson, Nathalie F. Anderson, David Lloyd, Kathryn Kirkpatrick, Mary O'Malley Madec, José Lanters, Joan FitzPatrick Dean, Donna Potts, Charles Fanning, Ann Neelon, Quitman Marshall, Ray McManus and Ed Madden. Thanks also to Kevin Higgins, Susan Miller DuMars, Jessie Lendennie, Siobhan Hutson, Paul O'Reilly, Pascale Guibert, among friends in the literary and publishing worlds in Ireland and France. During the spring semester of 2014 I was awarded the Heimbold Chair in

Irish Studies at Villanova University, and this opportunity provided the impetus to get me started on writing and revising this book. I wish to thank Professor Joseph Lennon for his hospitality while at Villanova. Over the years, my prose writing has been guided and improved by the skilled editors I have worked with: Thomas Dillon Redshaw and James Silas Rogers of *Eire-Ireland* and *New Hibernia Review*, and David Gardiner of *An Sionnach*. While writing and revising this book, David Gardiner's erudition and editing skills assisted me greatly. Again, I offer thanks to my family in Missouri and in Ireland for their continuing support for all of the many literary adventures that I have embarked on over the years.

The staff of the following libraries have assisted greatly as I searched for materials needed to complete this project: the Thomas Jefferson Library at the University of Missouri-St Louis; The Schlesinger Library at the Radcliffe Institute for Advanced Study at Harvard University; the James Hardiman Library at NUI Galway; the Falvey Memorial Library at Villanova University. I am also grateful to my superiors and colleagues at the University of Missouri-St Louis for their support, Dr Joel Glassman (Director Emeritus of International Studies & Programs) and Dr Frank Grady (Chair of English). Earlier versions of some of these essays appeared in anthologies and literary journals. I wish to thank Eamon Maher and Eugene O'Brien, editors of *Tracing the Cultural Legacy of Irish Catholicism: From Galway to Coyne and Beyond* (Manchester University Press, 2017) where 'Irish American Fables of Resistance' appeared; Catherine E. Paul, editor of *Writing Modern Ireland* (Clemson University Press, 2015) where 'The Use of Memory: Michael Coady's *All Souls*' was published; Siobhán Campbell and Nessa O'Mahony, editors of *Eavan Boland: Inside History* (Arlen House, 2017) where 'The Habit of Land: Eavan Boland's Irish American Voice' was first published. A much different version of 'Rory Gallagher's

Blues' was published in *An Sionnach* (Samhain/Fall 2005), edited by David Gardiner. Many thanks to Peter Moore and Geraldine Mills for their skilful indexing, and Viva Kathleen Momaday for her beautiful cover art. It has been a great pleasure working with Alan Hayes of Arlen House on this project and I am thankful for his enthusiasm and patience.

This book is dedicated to the memory, life and work of my great friend Philip Casey who passed away in 2018. I first met Philip at the Gorey Arts Centre in 1973 when our first poems were published in broadsheets edited by James Liddy. Philip Casey wrote the beautiful *Bann Trilogy* of novels as well as poems, plays and writing for children. A pioneer of digital media, he created *Irish Writers Online* in service to all Irish writers. When you have finished reading this book, please read Philip's books. Begin with *The Fabulists*, the first of the *Bann Trilogy*, and *Tried and Sentenced: New and Selected Poems*, both available through eMaker Editions.

NOTES

1   Rebecca Solnit, *A Book of Migrations: Some Passages in Ireland* (Verso, 2011, p. 9).
2   Neil Campbell, *The Rhizomatic West: Representing the West in a Transnational, Global, Media Age* (University of Nebraska Press, 2008, pp 1–2).

From Oven Lane to Sun Prairie: In Search of Irish America

'THE TRUTH ABOUT HIMSELF':
DEREK MAHON IN NEW YORK

New York breaks down America's founding myths, its various illusions, its airs of superiority and gestures of importance. Vibrant and unstable, the city reinvents American exceptionalism as multicultural variety. Driven by fiery vigor, New York is ever changing. We absorb, but hardly observe, renewal and reinvention, 'if you walked away from a place, they tore it down', as a character in Bernard Malamud's *The Tenants* observes.[1] And as crowds leave for the American interior, fresh faces push through JFK Airport bound for the five boroughs while others, more secretively, are deposited from vans on street corners – all eager for opportunity, embrace, stimulation, in a city where more than one hundred languages are spoken. Largely, and much to its credit, New York City resists the types of distinctions favoured by many American cities nowadays: legal/illegal, straight/gay, Christian/non-Christian, black/white, American born/foreign born, and so on.

   A long-standing entry way to the United States, New York has learned to accommodate the new arrival and inherited from its immigrants the lessons of impermanence: we are, all of us, merely passing through the city as we pass through our world. Move over on the bus! Make room on the subway bench for the new arrivals with whom we share our city! The new immigrant wears the city's face and the native-born reciprocates. Of course, New York is, in itself, exceptional: no matter where we live in the world, we look in its direction and hear, in even the most far-flung places, its murmurs. In addition to being a space, it is also a language, a film, a painting, a series of signs and signifiers, or a 'text', as Derek Mahon sees it.[2] It does not require personification.

As a result, we know many things about the city before disembarking at JFK, though we quickly learn that words and images can conflict with the now and the real. It is a space that the artist seeks to briefly occupy. My many-sided purpose here is to make note of Derek Mahon's presence in New York in the 1990s; to wade into his entanglements and seek to untangle some knots of his own creation and others attributed to him by commentators; and to describe the literary and personal triumphs that underline Mahon's New York odyssey. I am interested in the role Mahon plays in the diaspora, in adding some thoughts in support of what has been written by others, and in seeking to revise some key aspects of his life and work – alcohol addiction and confessional poetry in particular – that have been misunderstood. My work is indebted to scholars who have written on Mahon's work; to American critics of confessional poetics from M.L. Rosenthal to Gillian White; to Kay Redfield Jamison's biography of Robert Lowell; to scholars of addiction, Jim Lucey in particular; and to Edward Said and André Aciman, both writers of exile who also made their homes in New York. For Mahon, as for Muriel Spark, exile remains 'an inbred cultural dynamic',[3] that has followed him from place to place throughout his lifetime. For a period, New York became Mahon's substitute country in the same way as the sea became Joseph Conrad's. His work, its reception, its Irish and its American literary and cultural belongings, will serve as my roadmaps here. As an Irish writer in New York, Mahon is a man with a unique voice while, at the same time, belonging to a complex world that touches the local and the cosmopolitan.

Given its energy and global reach, it is hardly surprising that New York has fascinated foreign writers (visitors, immigrants or returnees like Henry James) as much as it has their American counterparts. For literary new arrivals, New York is a starting out point to life in America: the city is a confluence of brackish waters with the author resembling the otter – well able to prosper at points of convergence. Each new arrival adds his/her cultural nutrients to the city, thereby renewing both the city and nation. Here the new arrival is introduced to and prepared for American life. For some of us who settled in the old Irish Upper Manhattan enclave of Inwood in the 1980s, a first task was to learn Spanish, the *lingua franca* of the neighbourhood. New York is a safe place for the immigrant – we can cluster with faces from home in tightly-knit city corners without fear of being reported to I.C.E. by the NYPD. It is in these neighbourhoods that immigrants, among their own and at their own pace, assimilate – that is, become Americans. New York provides a fast-paced primer for America where the local and global connect. Given its seeming energetic disorder, the city might appear overwhelming to the newcomer; however, as Maeve Brennan reminds us, such factors are central to the city's personality:

> the lesson to be learned from these two encounters is that if everybody in the city were sorted out and set going in the right direction, New York would soon be a very quiet place.[4]

Here, chaos breeds innovation.

For over two centuries, Irish writers have passed through, settled in and written about New York, a pattern that continues today. Colum McCann's *Let the Great World Spin* (2009), Joseph O'Neill's *Netherland* (2008), and Colm Tóibín's *Brooklyn* (2009) are recent Irish and New York novels of wide readership and influence. Irish writers wear the city's faces and local writers reciprocate. Some of New York's notable writers are Irish Americans: Mary Gordon and Alice McDermott in *Final Payments* (1978) and *At Weddings and Wakes* (1992), respectively, write of other Irelands, in Queens and Brooklyn, where family homes are distinctive, American and Irish. To these novels we can add two recent Irish novels with New York settings: Mary Costello's *Academy Street* (2014) and Anne Enright's *The Green Road* (2015), as well as Jim Sheridan's film *In America* (2002). If we can say that Irish writers invented Ireland, then Irish Americans have done something of equal measure in New York.

A recent literary phenomenon has been Frank McCourt's *Angela's Ashes* (1996), the work of an author whose childhood straddled both sides of the Atlantic. In 1994, novelist Peter Quinn published *Banished Children of Eve*, his fictional recreation of Irish New York during the Civil War. A decade earlier William Kennedy's *Ironweed* (1983), the third installment of his Albany trilogy, had been published to great acclaim. Just as Irish writers situate work in America so too do Irish American writers look to Ireland – Alice McDermott's *Charming Billy* (1997) and Mary Pat Kelly's *Galway Bay* (2009) are good examples of this kind of reverse transatlantic drift. In poetry, Irish and American writers criss-cross the Atlantic and reveal areas of literary and linguistic belonging and disjunction. Among contemporary Irish poets in New York, no one has been more influential than Paul Muldoon, winner of the Pulitzer Prize for *Moy Sand and Gravel* (2002), whose work ranges widely across Irish and American spaces. On Broadway,

Irish America and Ireland have maintained an important presence through the work of John Patrick Shanley, author of *Doubt: A Parable* (2004), and Druid Theatre whose co-founder Garry Hynes became the first woman to be awarded a Tony for best director for Martin McDonagh's *The Beauty Queen of Leenane* (1996). To claim that the period from 1983 represents a diverse golden age of Irish American writing, a great deal of it being centred on New York, would not be to exaggerate. Of course, Irish Americans elsewhere in the US will claim that the work being produced in their locations is as vital as that which has emerged from New York, if less heralded.

Irish and American writers belong to the others' nation by reason of literary influence; engagements that pre-date setting foot in either the USA or Ireland. Wallace Stevens's assertion to Thomas McGreevy in 1948 is equally relevant in reverse and across time, 'Ireland is rather often in mind over here. Somehow the image of it is growing fresher and stronger'.[5] Influence, in the widest use of term, indicates deep and complex engagements born of birth, desire, loss, love, estrangement and material culture as well as books read, songs and tunes sung and heard, stories told and passed along. And influence is fluid and dynamic: just as New York does not stand still, so too its Irish-born writers are in motion, owing allegiance to multiple locations and subject to wide ranges of influences. Colum McCann, for example, is equally a Dublin and a New York writer while Tóibín is of Wexford, Barcelona and New York. Both New York and the works of McCann, Tóibín, Muldoon, Enright, Costello and others are literary confluences where many rivers of experience and influence have reached temporary fruition. One cannot read *Let the Great World Spin* without thinking of Don DeLillo's formal innovations in *Underworld* (1997) or *At Weddings and Wakes* (1992) without thinking of Joyce's mean style in *Dubliners* (1914).

In the past one sensed that Irish American and Irish writers moved in parallel universes; recently, formal, intellectual and thematic courses have moved toward closer alignment. If distance, influence and time have narrowed, the result has been an enlivenment of prose, poetry and drama. Contemporary Irish and Irish American authors show that one can inhabit more than one physical and literary space: most owe deep and long-lasting allegiances to multiple locations and languages. One need no longer simply be Irish or American or Irish American. To believe otherwise, in my view, is to adopt the pose of the ignorant backward individual and to fly in the face of the fluid nature of modern life. Irish and American writers have always read across national boundaries with the result that transatlantic influence has been vital and enabling. Even if a person spends their life in one place, they must adopt a wide lens. Ironically, the author will frequently reveal the flow of time and ideas by exploring lives lived in narrow places – a factor aligned in particular with Alice McDermott's achievement. Of course, the work located in a narrow space requires a broad vision that is at once local and cosmopolitan. Literary tradition, to recall T.S. Eliot's essay, has always been local, national, Anglophone and global.

That contemporary Irish poets have also written extensively about New York will be clear from Daniel Tobin's *Irish American Poetry from the Eighteenth Century to the Present*, and my focus here will be on the work of one of these poets: Derek Mahon's collection of poetry *The Hudson Letter* (1995) in particular. All discussions of Mahon's work must involve some exploration of textual instability. Just as New York is defined by flux, so too is Mahon's work. In the various volumes of selected and collected poems, published between 1991 and 2016, individual poems have been subject to systematic change. In 1991, Mahon noted that 'there is more where that came from', indicating that, going forward, revision of older work would have an important role to play in his writing life.[6]

The text of *The Hudson Letter* with the greatest provenance is what appears in the 2011 *New Collected Poems* where the title poem is renamed 'New York Time'. However, undercutting this is the fact that many of the poems included in the 1995 volume have been omitted from *New Collected Poems* (2011) indicating that *Collected* undermines itself by brazen omission. One poem from the first half of the original volume, 'The Travel Section', is inserted into *The Hudson Letter/New York Time* sequence where it replaces 'Sneakers' as part 7, among other changes. Co-published in 2016 by Gallery Press and Faber and Faber, *New Selected Poems* includes four sections from 'New York Time' and two from 'Decadence' (65–78). In the original 1995 volume, *The Hudson Letter* sequence comprises the book's second part with the opening section featuring a collection of translations, versions, light verses and lyrics as well as 'The Yaddo Letter', a verse letter to the poet's children that introduces aspects of form, theme, tone and voice that also govern *The Hudson Letter* sequence. Though it is best practice to follow the poet's hand and intentions with regard to the revision and framing of work, one cannot but be drawn back to the original *The Hudson Letter* (1995) given how much it captures its own moment of lived experience and composition, and how it demands, both in terms of time and text, to be seen as *the* original unit. *The Hudson Letter* (1995) corresponds more fully to Mahon's original desire to write a New York book in contrast to the 'New York Time' sequence that is concealed in *New Collected Poems* (2011). Has it been edited down so that it can be accommodated within the various collected and selected that serve as narratives of Mahon's life as a poet? Throughout literary history, such textual issues surface periodically, most notably with respect to Wordsworth's *The Prelude* and Whitman's *Leaves of Grass*. Here, I will continue to loop backward to the 1995 *The Hudson Letter* because it is where the work is assembled in its most complete form: it is a book whereas in *New Collected Poems* and *New Selected Poems* it has the appearance of being an abstract. Reviewing *New Collected Poems* Michael Hinds has rather cleverly noted the excitement that Mahon's revisions create, but also the futility of the task given that scholars will eventually take ownership of the work and undo Mahon's curation:

> As a book-event, Mahon's *New Collected Poems* is immediately impressive, riskily ignoring the arrangements of Mahon's earlier books in favor of making something new; this does not generate the epitaphic aura of a deathbed edition, therefore, but rather promotes the poet as the most effective moderator of his own work, at least as long as he lives. The very things that Mahon has removed are the things that scholarship will posthumously restore, of course, but to dismiss what he is doing in this book as somehow irresponsible or sad is off the mark; if Mahon is engaging in plastic surgery, it is at least self-administered, another wrangle with the limits of his own authority.[7]

Mahon's views are both lofty and pragmatic:

> revision is about past failures – failures of inspiration and expertise, and also the personal failure. We rehabilitate ourselves in language; to change a word or a line is to tweak the soul.[8]

Rehabilitation plays an important role in Mahon's literary practice while also being a central thematic element of *The Hudson Letter*. The poet seeks to rebuild a life that has gone off the rails, primarily as a consequence of an addiction to alcohol.

Ironically, by the time *The Hudson Letter* appeared in 1995, Mahon had already returned to Dublin where he was working on *The Yellow Book*. As is often the case in literature, the moment of the poems has passed before they are published, as experience and composition give way to publication and distillation. As David Lehman has pointed out, the New York School of Poets, for example, had dispersed before the term was familiar to readers.[9] Over the past few decades, *The Hudson Letter*, in its various iterations, has received a great deal of critical attention, not all of it favourable. Peter McDonald was quite dismissive; however, as time has passed scholars have warmed to the work. McDonald wrote shortsightedly of *The Hudson Letter* and *The Yellow Book* – the collection that followed it:

> *The Yellow Book* caused many of Mahon's admirers some embarrassment: owning up to disliking these poems, after all, seemed dangerously close to saying that one was bored by their author. *The Yellow Book* continues, and perhaps intensifies, the embarrassment. While those who enjoyed *The Hudson Letter* will enjoy this new volume, those who value Mahon for something other than his role as another talking head in the gallery of eminent Irish men of letters will experience again a familiar disappointment.[10]

Since then, Hugh Haughton, Terence Brown, Stephen Enniss, Patrick Crotty, Kelly Sullivan, Elmer Kennedy-Andrews, among others, have written extensively on *The Hudson Letter* with the result that we now have a more nuanced understanding of the sequence's triumphs and flaws. The poetics of *The Hudson Letter* in particular have been impressively detailed by these commentators while its weaknesses are best defined by John Redmond:

> the level of inconsistency in his verse-letters raises to an extreme one characteristic of much of his poetry and dramatizes a struggle which characterizes the whole of his poetry, the struggle between low-key observation and visionary grandeur.[11]

Arguably, some of the best recent Irish Studies literary scholarship is work focused on Mahon's recent poetry, a testament to its quality and complexity.

In addition to exploring aspects of *The Hudson Letter* that others have detailed – place, verse letters, autobiography, form – I am also interested in looking at the work more speculatively, and from some aspects that have been misunderstood or undervalued by others in the hope that I can broaden our view of the sequence and revise some of the ideas that I find problematic. While I will seek to place the volume within the context of Irish poetry, I also wish to look at it from the perspective of American confessional poetry and how American scholars have responded to it across the decades, and as a work written by an immigrant and alcoholic, and to see it more as a triumph over adversary rather than as the work of a partially down-and-out Irish misfit – a view promoted by some Mahon scholars, and by Mahon himself to some degree. Also, as Kelly Sullivan has pointed out, *The Hudson Letter* marks something of a turning point in Mahon's work as it 'initiates his environmental politics', one that would play a strong role in the work to follow.[12] Though an urban book, *The Hudson Letter* can also be read ecocritically: what Anne Fogarty writes of Joyce's Dublin can also be applied to Mahon's New York:

> Indeed, it is the very resistance of Joyce's works to pastoralism and conventional nature writing that makes them so amenable to contemporary ecocritical scrutiny, many of whose principal debates they anticipate. As several critics have noted, second-wave ecocriticism has questioned the very notion of nature as a thing apart, endowed with purity. They point to the fact that the natural is very often a human concoction or projection, and that it frequently merges with or is overlaid by the built and man-made environment. Further, many have made the case that it is more pressing to take account of urban, degraded and polluted landscapes and the sullied slums and back-streets occupied by the poor and the outcast in the modern metropolis than to continue to hanker after comforting notions of pristine natural spaces or of untouched wilderness.[13]

Mahon, like Pope, engages with and celebrates the city. As an environment, it is as alive as a rural landscape, worthy of his interest and it draws his praise. Sullivan, like Redmond, seeks to place *The Hudson Letter* within Mahon's whole body of poetry rather than thinking of it as an aberration.

Though usually employed and always housed in New York, Mahon, as Stephen Enniss, Hugh Haughton and others point out, lurches from one crisis to another and sees himself as a kind of outcast from country, home, family and employers. But he belongs in New York where many new arrivals are also, like him, figures cast off from their homelands – often traumatised and at wit's end. Mahon walks with immigrants along the streets and avenues, though also as a literary man who follows in the footsteps of Alfred Kazin and Frank O'Hara, authors of *A Walker in the City* and *Standing Still and Walking in New York*, respectfully. In his own wretched state, Mahon can note how his own demons correspond to and separate from those who are also afflicted:

> Here I was, sitting quietly in my studio
> and grading papers with the radio low
> as Pascal says we should, when out of the blue
> last night, under the fire-escape, some psycho
> sends up a stream of picturesque abuse
> directed, evidently, at my 4th-floor window,
> his reasoning trenchant, complex and abstruse –
> one of those paranoids who seem to know
> the system's out to get them even so;
> for paranoia, of course, is no excuse.[14]

Both interior and outer spaces are in turmoil. At the same time, like the process Sinclair Lewis initiated in such novels as *Babbitt*, Mahon is an author who has settled for a brief period in a city and he will depart when his work has been completed. Unlike Lewis who developed fictions in such locations, albeit featuring thinly-disguised people with whom he had become acquainted, Mahon wrote more autobiographically. Though he will leave New York for Dublin and then settle more permanently in Kinsale, a location suited to more traditional and sedate environmental thought, Mahon's deepening ecological conscience and aesthetic will have been renewed in New York as Kelly Sullivan has detailed. *The Hudson Letter* has the feel of a documentary, an often profane *tableau vivant* on steroids, with which the poetic temperament and body must strive to keep pace:

> 'Shut that fuckin' door!' 'Shit, man.' 'Colorado.'
> 'Hey, Joe! – Another Gibson, Scotch on the rocks
> and a mineral water for our friend.' 'No shit.'
> 'Myself, I've never been the marrying kind.'
> 'The smartest men in the States.' 'Get outa here.'
> 'That's 26 for Wake Forest, 18 for Notre Dame;
> Durcan replaces Heaney.' 'Don't pay no union dues.'[15]

If the city resists facile decoding, it shouts for in-tune description; therefore, to map part of downtown New York, and his own distraught mental state, are tasks that Mahon sets for himself. Of course, John Berryman had come to Dublin a few decades earlier with a similar purpose. By way of contrast, in 'Rising Late', a recent poem written from Kinsale, the body is static though the imagination forges ahead, albeit at a more graceful pentameter:

> Sun on the eyes, clear voices, open window,
> birdsong; ponies clop by on the road below.
> Whine of a chainsaw, the recurrent roar
> of power tools from a building site next door
> with crashing, rumbling, safety beep and buzz.
> A seagull shadow flickers; harbour noise;
> a honking coaster backs out from the quay.
> Enter a fly, the vast breath of the sea.[16]

Both Kinsale and New York can be in uproar, though one is more likely to be unhinged by it in the latter. In many of the poems in *The Hudson Letter*, distraction is a product of a harsh environment, whereas in 'Rising Late' the vista outside of the poet's room is mixed (birdsong and power tools); in fact, in 'Rising Late', disjunction is an aspect of the poet's style, his use of punctuation in particular, rather than a response to external stimuli and inner turmoil. In New York the city exercises control. In Kinsale the author observes and navigates sensory experience through a high window. In New York he is at work; in Kinsale he is more retired, though both are active imaginative states. Coincidentally, while Mahon was framing his work by taking New York walks, Tim Robinson was at home in Ireland making his own traverses of Árainn and Connemara. Both men were strangers to the places that engaged them. In Kinsale the speaker of 'Rising Late' is sitting and standing rather than walking, or standing still and walking as Frank O'Hara phrased it.

As D.G. Williams has pointed out, Mahon follows other poets from the classical period to the present – Horace, Ovid, Pope, Elizabeth Bishop, for example – in his use of the verse letter as the framing device for *The Hudson Letter*. Such epistles, Williams notes, 'are familiar and confessional' though they also 'tackle lofty and moral issues'.[17] In *The Hudson Letter* both aspects are represented:

> Today, across 3,000 miles of water
> and five time zones, my own prayer for my daughter
> would be, not innocence and ceremony
> exactly, but a more complicated grace,
> the sort of thing you play when you're alone,
> Katie, something slow and meditative,
> some rich myth of reconciliation
> as if a statue moved and began to live –
> for I like to think all this is a winter's tale.[18]

The address to his daughter is personal and intimate while at the same time speaking to such relationships in more lofty and abstract tones. It is particular to one daughter and general in its exploration of father-daughter relationships through time. Throughout the sequence, depending on context and theme, the voice alternates between one that is both formal and intimate, as in the previous quotation, and another that is quite loose:

> I go night-shopping like Frank O'Hara I go bopping
> up Bleecker for juice, croissants, Perrier, ice-cream
> and Gitane *filtre*, pick up the laundry, get back
> to five (5!) messages on the answering machine
> from Mary K. and Eliza, Louis, Barry and Jack,
> and on TV sixty channels of mind-polluting dreck.[19]

Here is a lovely imitation of the Frank O'Hara 'I do this, I do that' poetic of such *Lunch Poems* as 'Steps' and 'The Day Lady Died'. In *The Hudson Letter*, Mahon takes on board the styles, airs and shapes of other poets who have New York roots – Whitman, Bishop, Crane, Ginsberg, Auden – in a manner that is quite similar to how John Berryman absorbed much from Yeats and other Irish writers when he came to Dublin to complete his *Dream Songs* in the 1960s. Both poets pay homage to the 'majestic shades' that are, simultaneously, the heart and backdrop of their adopted cities.[20] Of course, it helped Mahon that he was teaching these poets to students while residing in New York and writing *The Hudson Letter*. The dialogue that Mahon enters into with these poets, as well as with Yeats when he addresses his daughter, is perhaps another kind of letter writing of one poet to others who have also meditated on this urban space and on some of these themes. As Mahon wrote for *The Irish Times* in 1993:

> The city as text ... The notion, though equally applicable to Dublin, London, Paris or LA (see Joyce, Dickens, Proust and Raymond Chandler), seems especially appropriate to the literary character of New York – as if, every block a quotation, the city were somehow destined to end up as a book. Perhaps it's one already: *Brightness Falls*? *The Bonfire of the Vanities*? No wonder they're getting out. Still, 'in America,' says the art critic Robert Hughes, 'nostalgia for things is apt to set in before they go'.[21]

In addition to addressing his readers, Mahon is also entering into a dialogue with New York's literary history.

Robert Cowan has pointed out in relation to Horace that:

> letters are a very private and personal form of communication between two individuals, whose content can be determined by the specific purpose of the correspondence but may also ramble through the topics which the writer wishes to discuss without the concern for formal unity or cohesion that literary texts tend to demand[22]

and these loose paths are followed by Mahon. For both writers, the epistle is a private work that is intended for wide sharing and it will need to ramble to keep the reader interested and to establish its often casual rather than more strictly formal tone. Also, in writing the *Epistles*, Horace was countering 'an adapted form of Stoicism [that] was extremely popular in Rome, since many of its ideals of the restraint of emotion, endurance, and public service' are ideas and strategies that he faulted.[23]

Until the publication of *The Hudson Letter* Mahon, as MacDonald makes clear, was a darling of the new critics and formalists, but the many rough edges that are part of the sequence's structure unnerved some of his readers, and remain part of the critical debate surrounding his work. While he has never strayed far from traditional poetic structures, preferring to seek innovation within these structures rather than outside of them, Mahon, in *The Hudson Letter*, challenges the notion that emotion must or can be willfully restrained in response to the often dire state of his own life, the city he was living in and his sense that the world was going to ruin as the end of the century approached. In this respect, his political outlook echoes that of Horace who wrote *The Satires* and *Epistles* 'in the course of some of the largest political changes which Rome ever underwent'.[24] In each case, literary form is matched to the poet's particular circumstances at the time of composition.

As Cowan points out, Horace's ideology in the *Epistles* is willfully inconsistent, and so is Mahon's in *The Hudson*

Letter. Mahon's feelings of being cast adrift and emotionally homeless in *The Hudson Letter* and how he explores these states find mirror images in Horace's 'Epistle I':

> I store up and organize material so that I may be able to draw upon it before long. And should you happen to ask who is my leader and whose house offers me shelter, there's no master I'm bound to swear loyalty to, and wherever the weather drives me is where I seek a roof.[25]

Though Mahon is gainfully employed in New York, for the most part, teaching and 'grading papers', his deeper loyalties lie elsewhere.[26] In Horace's and Mahon's cases, personal circumstances force both poets to adapt new poetics. Even though Mahon's sequence is highly autobiographical, we should also take heed of what Cowan refers as the 'authorial voice or persona', when considering Horace's *Epistles*, and not lose sight of the fact that the voice who speaks to us in the poem is a creation of the author's. An irony in all of this, as Kennedy-Andrews points out, is that Mahon is using the epistolary form, implying that he is writing from home, while, simultaneously, presenting himself as being homeless though this, too, establishes distance between speaker and poet.

Hugh Haughton has mapped *The Hudson Letter*'s structure and intent in this way:

> Weighing in at almost 1,000 lines long, it turned into Mahon's most ambitious poem to date. If the compositional and biographical time was multiple, however, it was conceived of as a poem set in a single day, St. Brigid's day or Imbolc, February 1st, the beginning of spring in the Celtic calendar. Written in eighteen sections, it takes us through a single day and on a journey across Greenwich Village from West to East Manhattan (with a detour via Laforgue on American pastoral and another, via Bishop, to Key West). In expanding the poem, Mahon mapped his personal home 'fixation' against a larger cultural stage, setting his personal crises against a bigger crisis of 'homelessness' in many senses.[27]

In his *Paris Review* interview with Eamon Grennan, conducted in New York during the period when *The Hudson Letter* was being planned and written, Mahon notes:

> I think one writes a different kind of thing, which is where I am now. I think that I have probably entered that middle-age stretch in which, so they say, you have the choice between falling silent or rambling on. Now, I won't ramble on, I know that. I think the pattern that's emerging is a general sort of silence punctuated by sudden bursts of noisiness. Aside from translation, I haven't produced a lot of verse in recent years. For some fairly obvious reasons, I think – all kinds of displacements, an inability to concentrate, distractions.[28]

As Haughton and Enniss detail, the near decade that passed between the publication of *Antarctica* and *The Hudson Letter*, was a period of great crisis for Mahon: his marriage broke up; he was frequently hospitalised for alcoholism; he was finding it difficult to write verse, all the while seeking employment.

Though they are explored by scholars in the various critical studies of *The Hudson Letter*, three intersections merit renewed attention because they allow us to contextualise the work more fully: Mahon's debt to American confessional poetry; issues related to his alcohol abuse and efforts at recovery while in New York; and his status as an immigrant in America. M.L. Rosenthal is credited with coining the term 'confessional' in an article published in *The Nation* in 1959.[29] Adam Kirsch explains this impulse more fully:

> What does it mean for a poet to tell the truth about himself? For American poets of the last half century, the answer has been found above all in a single-book: Robert Lowell's *Life Studies*, published in 1959. Before *Life Studies*, the standard account has it, poets of Lowell's generation were strapped in a corset of literary orthodoxy; after its revelations of mental illness and family trauma, they could breathe freely. Confessional poetry, as it came to be known, learned from

Lowell that modernist allusions and ambiguities are less important than simple, searing honesty.[30]

However, to counter the notion that equates confessional poetry with underwhelming verse, Kirsch reminds us that even when 'he seems most directly confessional, it is Lowell's artistry – which is also to say, his artificiality – that makes him a great poet'.[31] In 'Skunk Hour', that famous poem that closes out *Life Studies*, Lowell moves most indirectly towards his confessional moment:

> One dark night,
> my Tudor Ford climbed the hill's skull;
> I watched for love-cars. Lights turned down,
> they lay together, hull to hull,
> where the graveyard shelves on the town ...
> My mind's not right.[32]

It is confessional poetry, but it is also carefully crafted and skilfully-balanced verse.

Lowell's work had always been available in Ireland and he had long enjoyed a stellar reputation among Irish poets alongside Berryman and Roethke, all major confessional poets of this period who spent time in Ireland. When Mahon first arrived in Boston in 1965, he recalls:

> the other thing I was conscious of was the Harvard dimension – there were people about who had just a year or two previously been taking writing classes with Robert Lowell. So there was a lot going on. The American poetic psyche was very active.[33]

This is a sure indication of Mahon's familiarity with Lowell's work and influence. Even before his initial trip to the US, Mahon had inherited from Lowell a template for future use, a formal and aesthetic place to go to when the time came for him, decades later, to explore his own struggles and hospitalisations in his poetry, as Hugh Haughton has illustrated.[34] 'Skunk Hour' is one confessional example from *Life Studies* and 'Waking in the Blue' and 'Home After Three Months Away' are two even more powerful representations of Lowell's struggles with mental illness and the toll that this took on his family life. Lowell's bi-polar illness, like Mahon's alcoholism, set him on self-destructive trajectories that resulted in the fractures of many relationships.

Kirsch recounts Allan Tate's reaction to reading the manuscript of *Life Studies*:

> he recognized that Lowell had made a profound break with his early style and principles, and he was appalled. 'All the poems about your family,' he wrote Lowell, '… are definitely *bad*. I do not think that you ought to publish them'.[35]

This reaction parallels Peter McDonald's response to *The Hudson Letter*. Famously, Tate's instincts were proven wrong and his advice went unheeded. The formal transformation that Lowell had undergone to write *Life Studies* as he did, by setting aside rigid new critical orthodoxy and turning away from his masters, was extreme and brave, 'when I began to publish', Lowell noted, 'I wrote literally under the rooftree of Allen Tate. When I imitated him, I believed I was imitating the muse of poetry'.[36] Both Tate and Lowell understood the confessional impulse to be at cross purposes with new critical poetics: for Tate the necessity was to forsake confession while for Lowell the imperative was to invent a new poetics that would deliver 'the truth about himself' to readers.[37] Elmer Kennedy-Andrews finds:

> a remarkable duplication in the careers of Mahon and Robert Lowell. The ten-year gap between Mahon's *Antarctica* (1985) and his next major collection *The Hudson Letter* (1995), due at least partly to his alcoholism, repeats the ten-year gap in Lowell's career, also related to the poet's personal problems …

and the work published after these fallow periods is seen as being different with regard to subject matter, poetics and voice.[38]

Formally, Mahon appears to stick with what he knows best in *The Hudson Letter*:

> I've often filled a page with free verse, and I've thought, now that's not a bad piece of free verse, and it's hung around for a while. But eventually I throw it out, because it's not interesting to me. A thing has to have shape, profile, it has to clear its throat, make its presence felt, make itself visually interesting and so on. This is simply the way that I understand poetry.[39]

Mahon's transformation is thematic and linguistic rather than strictly formal though new language and themes undermine traditional form obliquely. Neil Corcoran sees in the verse letters 'irregularly rhyming loose pentameters, rather than octosyllabics, although the form does occasionally permit a short run of tetrameters'.[40] Relative to his earlier work, these new verse letters are in diction and syntax unrestrained so as to reflect New York exteriors and personal crises rather than Dutch interiors. The poetics of *The Hudson Letter* are also more hybrid American, Gotham City, melting pot. Robert Phillips has noted, writing of the American confessional poets, that 'openness of language leads to openness of emotion. For decades American poets seemed afraid of emotion'.[41] For Lowell, Snodgrass, Sexton, Plath, Berryman, and the poets of their generation, the subject matter they felt compelled to explore – mental illness among them – required new strategies that undermined the 'Eliotic aesthetic'.[42]

Similarly, when Mahon chose to write of such issues as hospitalisations for alcoholism, marital breakdown and his overwhelming sense of being set adrift in a demented New York, his viewpoint, language and structure required a major degree of change in order for the literary treatment of these inelegant states of being to be believable. At the same time, looking at his work from outside as a new reader, one might conclude that *The Hudson Letter*, in keeping with Neil Corcoran's description of its poetics, is a pretty traditional text. Mahon's harshest critics have misunderstood these poems believing that they have been undermined by laziness; in fact, what Mahon succeeds in achieving in *The Hudson Letter* is reinvention. His critics, perhaps, would have been happier had these calamitous events in his personal life not occurred at all, as Mahon himself would certainly have been elated by such a scenario; however, they did occur and fresh modes were required to respond to them in writing. Phillips reminds us that:

> the confessional is an anti-elegant tone whose candor extends even to the language in which poems are cast. The language of the confessional poem is that of ordinary speech, whether in blank verse or free, rhymed or not.[43]

In Britain and Ireland many scholars and commentators would prefer that poetry remain hyper-elegant while belonging to a world that can be harsh, divided, dysfunctional, violent and painful. Poetry, Lowell and his contemporaries remind us, should reflect in its forms and language the real world we inhabit rather than one we would prefer that existed: ours is a world of the dinner party and drawing room but it is also the world of the maternity hospital, the prison, the cafeteria and the gutter. Living in New York and adapting American confessional poetry to his own ends helped bring Derek Mahon back to life. Of course, there is a willful untidiness at the heart of Mahon's sequence though it is something that reflects, in a deliberate and artful manner, the work's location and its author's state of mind.

In her study of Mahon's generation of Northern Irish poets, Heather Clark highlights a devotion to traditional form that he shared with Longley, Muldoon and Heaney. And, in a part of his *Paris Review* that did not appear in the published version, Mahon voiced a withering view of American confessional poetry as nothing more than 'formless exhibitionism, like the worst of Anne Sexton; it's not poetry; it's not even readable'.[44] But such an attitude does not negate the confessional nature of *The Hudson Letter*; rather, these thoughts voiced while the sequence was being composed represent a poet's warning to himself regarding the pitfalls present in such an undertaking.

In many respects, the poet of *The Hudson Letter* is closely aligned with Louis McNeice, his most important literary mentor, who was also 'a poet struggling to find a home and a voice in two cultures, permanently displaced, permanently transient', though Mahon's is one more radically fashioned to New York, its place of composition.[45] Furthermore, centred on New York, rather than on America, *The Hudson Letter* is a work of literary regionalism influenced by John Hewitt, 'in poetry, regionalism manifested itself through placenames, idiomatic speech, rural or working class dictions, and translations from Irish legends'.[46] Though it required some linguistic and structural reformation on Mahon's part, the New York sequence is like a regional Ulster Renaissance text, being full of placenames, idiomatic speech, New York diction and Big Apple fables. Beneath its warped and glossy surface, *The Hudson Letter* is not quite as unusual as it might seem at first glance. On a more basic level, it is an act of translation – the lore, literature, personality, popular culture and poetry of the Old World translated for the New World and vice versa.

The psychotherapist Eileen Simpson, author of *Poets in Their Youth: A Memoir*, who had been married to John Berryman and who counselled Derek Mahon in his efforts to quit drinking and turn his life around during this period, recounts an anecdote that Saul Bellow told her concerning Delmore Schwartz, another poet who had fallen on hard times and the focus of his novel *Humboldt's Gift*, 'the man, who as Saul said, drew his writing "out of his vital organs, out his very skin, had nothing left to draw on"'; Mahon, in contrast, had much to draw on and has continued to enjoy a few most productive recent decades since departing New York.[47] Schwartz, unfortunately, perished. It is also interesting to compare Mahon's New York poems with Elizabeth Bishop's Brazilian work. Mahon is an admirer of Bishop's work and her poetry also becomes more autobiographical while she is unmoored from home as she takes 'part in her generation's common movement toward a more self-revelatory and autobiographical style'.[48] Like some of the critics of Mahon's New York period, Kirsch judges Bishop's Brazilian poems to be somewhat underwhelming. Clearly, as both Adam Kirsch and Robert Phillips are keen to point out, the confessional mode, even in the hands of the best poets, does not always provide satisfying results. Kirsch delivers harsh judgements on Lowell's *The Dolphin* and John Berryman's *Love + Fame* to illustrate this view. Considering Delmore Schwartz's career, Kirsch, like Eileen Simpson referring to Bellow, writes, 'as told by Saul Bellow, in the novel *Humboldt's Gift*, his life is a cautionary tale about the fate of the artist in commercial America'.[49] The fate of art, the artist, and planet has long been one of Mahon's own larger subjects. Mahon has managed to survive and thrive.

Gillian White's recent study, *Lyric Shame: The 'Lyric' Subject of Contemporary American Poetry*, casts some new light on confessional poetry and how it has been both embraced, discarded and absorbed into contemporary American poetic practice alongside the more traditional views of Wimsatt, Tate and others, while also being challenged by recent titans like Charles Bernstein, Marjorie Perloff and others – writer/scholars who favour more postmodern modes, L-A-N-G-U-A-G-E poetics for example and who oppose both traditional formalism, confessional poetry and other approaches. Also, as White points out, the American confessional mode has been under severe attack from the new formalism promoted by MFA programmes set up to professionalise the production of poetry, 'this culture determined in large part how poets were trained, how they would work, what they would read, and how they would write and publish'.[50] To these programmes, White ascribes sinister Orwellian motives where the emphasis is on recruitment of students, the hiring of faculty, the creation of bureaucratic mazes and the mass production of cookie-cutter poets/poems rather than on more germane issues such as quality, not to mention vision and imagination. Even though Mahon taught creative writing in New York and at Trinity College Dublin, he expressed little enthusiasm for the task, preferring to take students through literature's notable works. White provides an interesting analysis of Brooks' and Wimsatt's influence, scholars who claimed that 'once we have dissociated the speaker of the lyric from the personality of the poet, even the tiniest lyric reveals itself as drama', we begin to appreciate poetry at a deeper level.[51]

For Mahon, given the material he sought to explore and his sense of being in crisis at the time, it would have been impossible to disassociate the speaker of *The Hudson Letter* from the poet; hence his use of the more familiar Horatian verse epistle which allowed for a merger of the poet and speaker. In this regard, as John Redmond points out, he was always following Auden's example. Some readers, enamoured of Mahon's lyric gift, failed to recognise, or refused to do so, the necessity for this formal shift. Instructively, running parallel to the resistance of some commentators to Mahon's New York work, is White's revising of her own resistance to Anne Sexton's poetry:

> I was acutely aware that I should dislike Anne Sexton's poetry long before I ever read a single Sexton poem ... One might say that if Bishop is for some people the 'most beloved' lyric poet, Sexton is everybody's least beloved lyric poet.[52]

When *The Hudson Letter* appeared, Mahon, for some readers, became Sexton – the sublime lyric poet who had written 'A Disused Shed in Co. Wexford', and other widely-anthologised poems, who had traded in elegance for disorder and brevity for length. At the same time, as Neil Corcoran notes, one is permitted to appreciate work from both phases of Mahon's career, the work published before and after *The Hudson Letter*:

> If the maudlin and the sententious are tones occasionally at least at the edge of earshot in the sequence, however, this kind of familial intimacy also serves to anchor it in the frayed anxieties, exacerbations, self-doubts and guilts of the quotidian in a way that willfully distresses the poised, melancholy perfectionism of earlier Mahon which, however one may admire it (and this critic admires it immensely), could hardly be expected, itself alone, to maintain viability throughout an entire career, even if the volume's predominantly negative or indifferent reviewers have thought otherwise.[53]

The shift manoeuvred in *The Hudson Letter* catches our attention, puts us off-guard and, ultimately, results in Mahon's work being more many-sided and more deeply engaging. His verse letters are 'willfully inconsistent' to reflect the mind of its author at the time and its location.[54] As Gillian White reminds us in relation to her own resistance to Sexton's work, we are sometimes called upon to leap across a chasm with an author; perhaps, despite our own first judgements. Mahon's life at that time was quite messy and of a complexity that the lyric could not accommodate. However, within this context, it should be noted that even Sexton revealed that the person who speaks in her confessional poems is an invention; similar conceits underline Horace's *Epistles* and Mahon's approach in *The Hudson Letter*. Adrienne Rich brings the personal and artistic into play when she says that 'we were trying to live a personal life ... the only way we could attest to'.[55] In other words, poets must adopt certain voices because they have to in order to bear honest witness. Though Mahon would have disagreed with many American poets and scholars on issues of where poetry might go and how it might be written, he was living in the midst of a diverse literary culture in New York with a consciousness that has always been tuned in to American literary voices.[56] America allows one to cast off one's inherited restraints. New York City, a capital of reinvention, calls out for such measures. Mahon was up to the task.

For the literary scholar, writing about a man who is both a writer and an alcoholic is unnerving. Yes, there have been some splendid studies of this topic in the Irish context, notably Anthony Cronin's *Dead as Doornails*, a work that explores the negative influence that drinking and involvement in a tavern-centred culture has had on writers, Irish for the most part, even though it is not the book's given subject. Among American studies, Tom Dardis's *The Thirsty Muse; Alcohol and the American Writer* and Eileen Simpson's *Poets in Their Youth* are worthy explorations of how canonical American authors have used and abused alcohol. Anecdotally, we might presume that writers like to drink and that a drinking culture informs a literary one and vice-versa. Even today at a safe distance from the various milieus of Dylan Thomas, Brendan Behan and Patrick Kavanagh, post-reading audiences and poets, more often than not, drift toward a bar: for generations, it has been the default location. One of Anthony Cronin's functions, and triumphs, in *Dead as Doornails* is how he demonstrates, without dogmatism, the limitations and shortcomings of the literary/drinking culture. Here, he recounts a late encounter with Patrick Kavanagh in McDaid's:

> One of the things that shocked and depressed me in Dublin was Kavanagh's condition. He was so thoroughly far gone in whiskey and for the most part he sat in McDaid's leaning forward with his head sunk, clutching his stomach, taking little or no part in the conversation around him.[57]

Through dire circumstances, work continued to be produced as Cronin notes in relation to Brendan Behan who, at a time when many considered him to be 'a write-off' because he appeared so idle and alcoholic, was engaged in writing *The Quare Fellow*, his major dramatic work.

The literary world as described by Cronin is largely Dublin based, the one that Mahon emerged from in Belfast and Dublin was defined by movement as poets meandered back and forth across the Atlantic, the Irish Sea and elsewhere. Just after Mahon's residency at Yaddo ended – the poem entitled 'The Yaddo Letter', dated April/May 1990, closes the first part of *The Hudson Letter* and precedes the eponymous sequence – he arrived in New York to take part in a series of readings that included Seamus Heaney, John Montague, Paul Muldoon, Medbh McGuckian and others at a time when, despite a recent hospitalisation, he was drinking heavily. On such visits, as Enniss points out, Mahon found refuge in The Lion's Head and the White Horse Tavern in New York. In one horrific and memorable scene that Enniss records, we observe Mahon and John Montague getting into an altercation with one another after a boozy evening spent in the ironically-named Kinsale Tavern:

> That night, Mahon insisted on making a chivalric show of drinking champagne out of a woman's slipper, at which point Montague helpfully ordered the necessary champagne. Later that evening Montague had to help him back to Richard Ryan's apartment where he was staying, only to have Mahon lash out at him angrily in a torrent of verbal abuse. Alcohol had made him emotionally erratic, and it was the kind of outburst that was becoming increasingly common.[58]

Many of Mahon's friends and acquaintances went to some lengths to help him get sober. In a recent essay, Mahon has sought to draw a map of his alcoholism: from the outset seeing it as 'an important feature of the writing life itself', among a variety of other linked possibilities.[59]

In my view, the skills the literary scholar develops do not easily translate into reading the life of a substance abuser. When one seeks to study issues related to alcohol and substance abuse, one begins to understand the range and scale of the problem; for one, research libraries have rows and rows of studies on these subjects as I noted myself when I went in search of expert views that might help me understand Derek Mahon's addiction to alcohol. Where does one start? Stephen Enniss, Mahon's biographer, provides many examples of his excessive drinking and identifies the various hospitalisations and interventions that have served as mile-markers during his life, including his time in New York. Drinking, unreliability, recovery, illness, time lost from work and malaise brought on by job responsibilities led to the loss of his teaching position at Queens' College in New York, as well as separation from family and a kind of semi-permanent homelessness for a number of years, all detailed by Enniss.

Stephanie Brown of the Stanford Alcohol Clinic prefaces her study of the subject with this statement:

> In this book, I side with the alcoholic – the alcoholic who is still drinking and the alcoholic who is sober. I am sympathetic to the alcoholic who mistrusts professional helpers and therefore believes that those who have not experienced alcoholism firsthand cannot understand or help the alcoholic. Although I am sympathetic, I also believe that the alcoholic badly needs the professional.[60]

I do think that while considering Mahon's alcoholism Enniss exercises some poor judgement. He catalogues Mahon's failures and shortcomings without seeking to contextualise them enough with the result that one might conclude that what happened to Mahon with alcohol is quite common for a person – man, woman or writer – born in Ireland. The poet that Enniss seeks to celebrate is reduced to something of an alcoholic Irish stereotype and caricature. It is an old trap. As Stephanie Brown sides with the alcoholic so too do we expect Enniss to side with his subject. We do not require hagiography from a biographer though we demand balance and context, particularly given how Irish people have so often been caricatured as drunks. Enniss enumerates on Mahon's binges and hospitalisations;

however, other than his reference to advice the poet received from the psychotherapist Eileen Simpson, he makes no deep effort to understand the disease and the treatments that play such a large role in his subject's life and work.[61] Instead, he would appear to accept alcoholism as a given ingredient of Mahon's literary, island culture – an unfortunate subtext of his biography. Without exploring alcoholism medically, Anthony Cronin, a recovering alcoholic himself, writes with greater empathy.

It is no longer good practice to ignore medicine and social science when considering the role that alcohol or substance abuse plays in the lives of authors – they do not live in vacuums and writers, and the scholars who offer commentary on their lives and work, sometimes 'badly need the professional' to be cured or informed, or both. When literary scholars explore the lives of men and women who are addicted to various substances, it behooves all of us to avail of the professional expertise that is available because literary educations have limits. In her review of *After the Titanic: A Life of Derek Mahon*, Christina Hunt Mahony concludes that 'the writing in this volume does not sustain a level suited to its subject' and she lays much of the blame 'at the feet of the publisher', who, one suspects, did not provide proper counsel, editorial advice and copy-editing service to Enniss.[62] She goes on to fault the portrait of Mahon that emerges in the biography because:

> there is not enough of the wit, resilience, and exuberance for life, that is present, at times luminous, in [Mahon's] writing no matter how depressed or miserable Mahon was at the time of composition.[63]

Enniss's biography leaves one with the impression that, even though Mahon has been a friend, son, husband, father and lover, he is little more than a cruel and savage misfit who has managed to write great verse. One is forced to read between the lines of the unfortunately-titled *After the Titanic: A Life of Derek Mahon* to uncover nuggets of the poet's generosity, kindness and wit.

One of the great joys in being alive at this moment in history, both in Ireland and in the United States, is in belonging to a society where to admit to difficulty and hardship in areas of mental health and addiction is no longer considered shameful; in fact, it is the opposite. For most of us we would rather help the alcoholic recover than recount his/her collapse without reference to its deeper context. We would prefer, as it were, to reach out a helping hand to an Edgar Allan Poe lying in the gutter in Baltimore than to return home and recount for others whom and what we had witnessed. Of course, in context, we can do both.

Among Irish American New York contemporaries of Mahon's are at least two authors who have detailed their struggles with alcohol in memorable works: Pete Hamill's *A Drinking Life* and M.G. Stephens's *Where the Sky Ends: A Memoir of Alcohol & Family*. To better understand his own addiction, Stephens provides lucid medical and family narratives and reportage:

> I remember one of those medical lectures we received when I was a patient at Smithers Alcoholism and Treatment Center in New York about how alcoholics react differently to ether because it's a chemical whose molecular structure bears a resemblance to alcohol's. Because alcoholics metabolize alcohol differently than non-alcoholics do – which finally is all that an alcoholic is, a person with an allergy to booze – they react differently to ether than alcoholics do. I remember the Irish nurse at Smithers telling us that, working in operating rooms, she knew when she had an alcoholic on her hands, because he or she would wake up in the middle of an operation. Why? Because alcoholics need more anesthesia than non-alcoholics; they need enough to convince their bodies that the anesthesia is not ethyl alcohol, its friend and demon, its being and its all, the body's nemesis, its dark other.[64]

Neither Hamill nor Stephens is referenced by Enniss with the result that the wider contextual space Mahon inhabits as an alcoholic – beyond the literary one – is ignored.

Kay Redfield Jamison's recent biography of Robert Lowell takes an altogether different approach to the role played by illness in the life of a writer, and points to the road not taken by Enniss. Her study begins at the intersection of mental illness and creativity noting how Lowell, just emerging from the purple patch of writing that would result in *Life Studies*, 'was admitted to a mental hospital severely psychotic. It was his fifth psychiatric hospitalisation in eight years'.[65] Going further back, Redfield Jamison prefaces her work by returning to the 1856 admittance to a mental asylum of Harriet Brackett Spence Lowell, the poet's great-great grandmother, both mental illness and addiction trending to run in families. Lowell's behaviour and hospitalisations were painful to his friends and family, as he himself acknowledged in his poetry, but he:

> came back from madness time and again, reentered the fray, and kept intact his friendships. He kept his wit and his capacity to love. He went back to his work.[66]

Mahon, if we accept Hunt Mahony's understanding of his character, was also able to return from his hospitalisations and from the bouts of drinking that necessitated them, and renew friendships. He was never quite the hard-edged monster of Enniss's devising. Jamison makes the point that her book 'is not a biography' but rather 'a psychological account of the life and mind of Robert Lowell'.[67] In this regard, she is giving a kind of precedence to the role that Lowell's bipolar condition played in his life and work and her own training as a clinical psychologist specialising in 'the study and treatment of manic-depressive (bipolar) illness'.[68] It should be noted that this is not Jamison's first book on a literary subject; in fact, *Robert Lowell: Setting the*

River on Fire, notwithstanding the author's modest assessment, is indeed a biography in every sense.

Jamison makes reference to, and draws upon, Ian Hamilton's 1982 biography of Lowell, the first to appear, though she notes that 'its impact on Lowell's reputation as a poet and man was lasting and negative'.[69] Like Enniss, Hamilton, as Jamison notes, realised 'that irrational or shocking behavior makes better copy than the uses to which the turmoil is put and the discipline that shapes and constrains it'.[70]

What Richard Tillinghast, a former student of Lowell's and a distinguished writer in his own right, has said of Hamilton's biography might be equally true of Enniss's, 'Robert Lowell was notably unlucky in Ian Hamilton's major biography. [It was a] damagingly wrong-headed and skewed picture'.[71] With regard to Lowell's and Mahon's illnesses and addictions, perhaps Jonathan Raban's conclusion is the most apt in both cases: he describes Hamilton's biography as 'pitiless and strangely uncomprehending of his illness'.[72] The life of the wild and crazy alcoholic Irish writer needs no glorification nor should writers who happen to be alcoholics be subject to ridicule. Anthony Cronin has explored the tragic consequences of this aspect of the Irish literary world with intelligence and empathy, particularly in relation to the life and times of Patrick Kavanagh. Though Enniss' study is indispensable for the wealth of information it provides, its narrative drive to reveal Mahon as an Irish train-wreck poet is both sadly dated, highly offensive and reeking of the kind of last word superiority that Elizabeth Cook-Lynn, the great Lakota writer, has decried:

> no matter what happens in modern America, you know, nontribal people always think that they have the last word. They are the ones, they think, who are in charge of time and history.[73]

In his study, *The Life Well Lived: Therapeutic Paths to Recovery and Wellbeing*, Jim Lucey, an Irish psychiatrist, explores issues related to trauma, shame, guilt, pain and alcoholism – all under the general heading of mental illness. Considering Derek Mahon's situation in light of a case study, 'Robert and Barbara', we begin to understand the difficulties that Mahon faced in his battle to give up drinking. Though no one intervention is ideal or workable in all circumstances, Lucey finds that the Community Reinforcement Approach and Family Training (CRAFT) strategy to be most promising. Such an approach is founded on the necessity of including the alcoholic's larger family in the treatment process; however, in Mahon's case, such an undertaking would have been impossible because of his separation from family and as a result of his nomadic existence. Consciously or not, for a long time, Mahon was on the run from a cure and allowing himself fresh starts by settling briefly in other places, though eventually, particularly in relation to the loss of his position at Queens' College in New York, his demons and behaviours caught up with him. Not having his family to assist him was offset for Mahon by the loyalty of friends, students and colleagues who reached out to help him, as Enniss reveals. Had it been possible for Mahon to remain part of his family unit, as Lucey explains, he might have been able to begin recovery at an earlier date. His peripatetic existence at this time indicates that the cure was always chasing Mahon rather than the other way round.

Though Enniss's many accounts of Mahon's collapses and hospitalisations make for painful reading, Lucey's explorations allow us to see Mahon's life during this period contextually and more triumphantly. The sense of Mahon as a hopeless case is undercut by evidence cited by Lucey indicating that 'less than six percent of people with alcohol misuse enter into any effective treatment'.[74] Also, research indicates that 'mental health problems are not just for other people, or other families, or other races, or other genders – or other socio-economic groups: mental health difficulties intersect with everyone, everywhere', indicating that literary scholars and biographers should think of writer-alcoholics not just as a literary subset but as human beings who belong to larger humanity.[75] Dinesh Bhugra, president of the World Psychiatric Association, writes:

> that it is well recognized that one in four adults in their lifetime will develop a psychiatric disorder. Thus every family in the land will be affected directly or indirectly by the issues of mental health.[76]

Dryden equated madness with genius; however, modern psychiatry asks us to link writers with the rest of the populace rather than separate them from it, though, as Redfield Jamison points out in relation to Robert Lowell, a manic state may trigger a creative burst. Stephen Enniss's biography of Derek Mahon, at least for the present, defines the poet for his audience with his alcoholism and bad behaviour placed front and centre; however, as Lucey explains, to take such a tack is unfair and opposed by professionals:

> Mental health problems do not define who we are. They tell us about our human experience: things that have happened to us, and how we think, feel and behave as a result. Mental health issues are mostly transient and fluctuant.[77]

Though Enniss makes the point that Mahon is in recovery from his disease, the accounts he provides of the out-of-control poet are not deflated because positive revelations are delivered in a minor key. In New York, Mahon was in the process of attempting recovery and 'recovery is a testament to human resilience, and of the determination to heal and be healed', an indicator of the poet's triumph over adversity.[78]

Examining the idea of wellness in relation to men and woman, Lucey notes eight dimensions of wellness promoted by the Substance Abuse and Mental Health Services Administration (SAMHSA): 'emotional; environmental; financial; intellectual; occupational; physical; social; and spiritual'.[79] He argues that, although this is a complex subject, it would be difficult to eliminate any one of these from the list. Mahon was clearly under great stress while writing *The Hudson Letter*: emotional, environmental, financial, occupational and physical for certain. But Lucey also provides five indicators of robust mental health that can be seen as pathways 'to wellness: Connect; Be Active; Take Notice; Keep Learning; Give', all of which the Mahon of this period is possessed of in abundance. He connects with his environment, with his work and with others; he is active as a writer, teacher and friend; he takes notice of the world around him as we know from his poems and from his contributions to *The Irish Times* from New York; he continues to learn by absorbing from books and from the city, which is a text; and he gives back through his work. Mahon, like many, is able to 'learn even in an environment where [he experiences] reversal'.[80] What literary scholars have called 'confessional poetics' Lucey labels 'disclosure' and cites its importance:

> by being open about their panic attacks, anxiety, addictions or depression, these individuals do a great service. They increase the space for mental health conversation and so help to reduce the shame about these experiences.[81]

Of course, in order to begin his own process of recovery, Mahon needed to be open to his alcoholism as it was the trigger for much of the tribulation in his life. Along the way, in much of *The Hudson Letter*, disclosure becomes aligned with poetics. Given Mahon's regard for *Life Studies*, this was an easy shift for him to make, though one that some scholars have found hard to stomach. In life and in art he had to separate himself from some elements of his past or be destroyed. Since the publication of *The Hudson Letter*, Mahon has continued to renew himself as a writer and to demonstrate that the confessional and the poetic can go hand-in-hand. Reticent formalism is but one mode of writing and one strategy for viewing the world. Fortunately for Mahon, Lowell's *Life Studies* had given him the blueprint to tell 'the truth about himself'.[82] In *The Hudson Letter* Mahon invents a poetics of disclosure.

Though his coming to America to teach at a university has about it the ring of a coronation, Mahon's position is quite different to other arrivals from the North of Ireland such as Seamus Heaney's at Harvard and Paul Muldoon's at Princeton, for example. The university positions Mahon held were largely temporary in nature. At the same time, as we might traditionally think of it, Mahon does not remind us of the typical immigrant. He was a middle-aged man with an international reputation as a poet and not a school-leaver, refugee or laid-off factory worker though, like many who have sought refuge in America, he was fleeing a violent home country. Of course, America has for a long time been a haven for those who could not hack it at home or were escaping from familial discord or violence; therefore, Mahon's situation is not unlike that of many others.

Also, the nature of immigration has changed in recent times. Today, many immigrants are highly-skilled, well-educated and have multiple and complex loyalties to places: Mahon belonged, for example, to Ireland, North and South, England and to multiple languages. In recent decades, many Bosnians coming to the US as a result of the Dayton Accords have lingered for long periods of time in Germany awaiting resettlement. In Asia, refugees have had to endure long waits in transitional camps in in-between countries while being processed and vetted before being granted permission to immigrate into America. This same pattern has been played out elsewhere, most recently in Europe where countless thousands of refugees from

Syria, Iraq and elsewhere have been stalled in Italy and Greece while on their way, hopefully, to Germany.

We might think of immigration as a binary process that has brought individuals from one place to another – Ireland to the USA, for example – though even this view, though justifiable, is rather simplistic. Frequently in the nineteenth century and later, Irish people emigrated to England before then emigrating again to America; others went from Ireland to America to Mexico; while, even more exotically, Patrick Lafcadio Hearn, another Irish writer, emigrated from Ireland to America to Japan. Like Hearn and Mahon, human beings are capable of establishing deep roots in multiple places. In this regard, to label Irish Americans in Ireland as monochrome Yanks is to seek to reduce in scale what will be engaging and illuminating. In our contemporary map of the global world, one of Mahon's concerns in *The Hudson Letter*, loyalties are rarely permanent and immigration is no longer always the life sentence it once was. One can, like Mahon and many other Irish people, come to America and, after an interval, return to Ireland. Some might see in such lives evidence of commuting rather than emigration though this is a fallacy in my view because connections nowadays are often defined by the rhizome rather than the root. Even if one's emigration is finite, the émigré can still be subject to intense feelings of homesickness and displacement. Equally, such feelings can be spread widely across nationality, gender and socio-economic background. Mahon's own sense of displacement is private rather than national, cultural or environmental: in New York he is cut off from his family, his children in particular, though he is neither the first nor the last immigrant father sent to America to help support his family. In Mahon's case, his own sense of being displaced is compounded by the fact that he seeks to support a family structure that has collapsed.

One captivating aspect of *The Hudson Letter* is the intense level of Mahon's engagement with New York – from its high literary culture to its flotsam and jetsam. Writing of his own life as an immigrant in America, André Aciman, who was raised in Alexandria, notes that:

> Egypt is just the grid, the matrix, the cavity into which I 'throw back' my life long after leaving Egypt. My present is meaningless unless it is *thrown back* to Egypt.[83]

Even though Mahon does throw back his experiences in New York to seek some degree of register with what had been absorbed at home, he is also able to separate himself from the past. In part, this is possible because he had already spent time in America and knows that he is not under an immigrant life sentence. Aciman, on the other hand, is an Egyptian Jew whose community was erased by General Nasser and so no return is permitted. With regard to alcoholism, evidence does not suggest that Irish people are more likely to suffer from this disease than other immigrants:

> no clear association emerges from the studies of migration to the United States or of immigrant status across generations in relation to alcohol use, except for the case of Hispanic Americans. There is considerable variation across racial/ethnic groups.[84]

Lauer and Lauer argue that 'instead of asking what can be done for an alcoholic, you need to ask first what kind of alcoholic you are dealing with'.[85] If one puts Mahon's problems down to merely being Irish, one will never ask this question.

The Hudson Letter is a letter home from America that belongs to the literature of ordinary people and, for centuries, Irish immigrants have written these missives home. One collection of such letters is *Irish Immigrants in the Land of Canaan* (2003) – letters written between 1675 and 1815, mostly by settlers from Mahon's native Ulster. Describing these, the editors note that:

> in the process they were also creating images and constructing 'selves' for the edification of their correspondents or their posterity. Many of these 'performances' were ritualistic and yet intensely personal ... these testaments were public as well as private exercises.[86]

Here, unschooled letter writers provide long and richly-detailed accounts of life in another country, and this is a technique these authors share with the author of *The Hudson Letter*. Both the settlers' letters and Mahon's verse letters are rich in engagement and attitude with the sense that only by describing all on paper can America be revealed. *The Hudson Letter* is a work that negotiates on many levels; in particular, between the literary verse letter and the immigrant's more humble letter home. In part, this is what gives it its power and originality and underlines its mixture of formal and informal discourse and voice. In addition to belonging in the more rarified literary world, Mahon's representations of time spent in New York also belong to the more ordinary literature of the diaspora. Like the letters described by the editors of *Irish Immigrants in the Land of Canaan*, Mahon's work is a 'performance' created to appeal to his literary audience, but it is also designed to explain something of his life in New York to his children. Such performances and communications, like letters written in prose or verse, were intended to be quickly read and readily understood, notwithstanding their other levels such as omission and part revelation, and could be undermined by unhelpful symbol and artifice. For his purposes, the epistle and the confession suited Mahon. Writing of Mahon's process before *The Hudson Letter*, Peter McDonald has noted 'that the poems have always gravitated towards a cold and unpeopled area which exists generally before, or after, anything ordinarily recognizable as historic process', one way of highlighting their more primalist aesthetic.[87] In New York, the poet observed 'the hissing chemicals inside the well-wrought urn; an urnful of explosives', which is one of Mahon's ways of describing his poetics of this period.[88]

Edward Said, another immigrant writer in New York, also found the internal structure of his own work altered by engagement with New York:

> It is the fact of New York that plays an important role in the kind of criticism and interpretation which I have done, and of which this book is a kind of record. Restless, turbulent, unceasingly various, energetic, unsettling, resistant, and absorptive, New York today is what Paris was a hundred years ago, the capital of our time ... This is not always a positive or comforting thing, and for a resident who is connected to neither the corporate nor the real estate nor the media world, New York's strange status as a city unlike all others is often a troubling aspect of daily life, since marginality, and the solitude of the outsider, can frequently overcome one's sense of habitually being in it.[89]

The Hudson Letter and *The Yellow Book* are work in a later style that anticipate the century's end. As New York changed, the old literary neighbourhood where Mahon lived and which was once, as Said notes, a centre for the small press and the indigent artist, became unaffordable as the wealthy, seeking to live in a cultural space, moved in and forced the artists out. Both Mahon and Said connect to a sense of history and culture, though it is one that is in decline, or has shifted elsewhere:

> Greenwich Village has also passed away as America's Bohemia, as have most of the little magazines and the artistic communities that nourished them. What remains is an immigrants' and exiles' city that exists in tension with the symbolic (and at times actual) center of the world's globalized late capitalist economy whose raw power, projected economically, militarily, and politically everywhere, demonstrates how America is the only superpower today.[90]

Seeking to make sense of his own sense of dislocation, and to shed light on how we might view Derek Mahon's, Said concludes:

> Adorno's reflections are informed by the belief that the only home truly available now, though fragile and vulnerable, is in writing ... To follow Adorno is to stand away from 'home' in order to look at it with the exile's detachment. For there is considerable merit in the practice of noting the discrepancies between various concepts and ideas that they actually produce. We take home and language for granted; they become nature, and their underlying assumptions recede into dogma and orthodoxy.[91]

Part of Mahon's story as a writer and intellectual has been his firm resistance to the assumptions that underline Irish literary, political and religious discourse. By rejecting his family's political dogma, he displaced himself before leaving Ireland and added to this by being separated from family and by placing himself in New York. Like Said, Mahon has found a home in writing. It offers continuity, promises a measure of control, disclosure and a path toward wisdom. It is my view that *The Hudson Letter* can only be fully understood for what it is when its context is enlarged to encompass its many literary and cultural contexts: classical, Irish and American. In addition to its literary merits, it is also a work of immigrant witness and a narrative of survival in the face of personal demons – on many levels triumphant. Concluding his incisive reading of the sequence, Hugh Haughton notes that while the work appears stable with regard to personal narrative and metrical form it is:

> fundamentally unstable, jagged, polyphonic ... If few readers have yet got to grips with its dizzying allusive complexity, its 'encoded mysteries' represent an extraordinary demonstration of the 'resilience of our lyric appetite' faced with a moment of personal and cultural crisis.[92]

To consider this in another context is to hear what Edward Said has said:

> Exile is never the state of being satisfied, placid, or secure. Exile, in the words of Wallace Stevens, is 'a mind of winter' in which the pathos of summer and autumn as much as the

potential of spring are nearby but unobtainable. Perhaps this is another way of saying that a life of exile moves according to a different calendar, and is less seasonal and settled than life at home. Exile is life led outside habitual order. It is nomadic, decentered, contrapuntal; but no sooner does one get accustomed to it than its unsettling force erupts anew.[93]

Setting *The Hudson Letter* at the beginning of February in New York when it is the opening of spring in Ireland but not in North America is to promote the notion of an alternative calendar, cartography, psyche, aesthetic and sense of belonging. Nothing about Mahon's sequence is satisfied, placid or secure.

NOTES

1   Bernard Malamud, *The Tenants: A Novel* (FSG, 1971), p. 8.
2   Derek Mahon, *Journalism: Selected Prose 1970–1995* (Gallery Press, 1996), p. 238.
3   *Ibid*, p. 179.
4   Maeve Brennan, *The Long-Winded Lady* (The Stinging Fly Press, 2017), p. 77.
5   Holly Stevens (ed.), *The Letters of Wallace Stevens* (Knopf, 1966), p. 586.
6   Hugh Haughton, *The Poetry of Derek Mahon* (Oxford University Press, 2010), p. 219.
7   Michael Hinds, '(Re)Writing', *Irish Literary Supplement*, Vol 32, No. 2, Spring 2013, p. 6.
8   Derek Mahon, 'Changing a Word', *Olympia and the Internet* (Gallery Press, 2017), p. 20.
9   David Lehman, *The Last Avant-garde: The Making of the New York School of Poets* (Doubleday, 1998), pp 19–30.
10 Peter McDonald, 'Incurable Ache', *Poetry Ireland Review*, 56, Spring 1998, p. 117.
11 John Redmond, 'Willful Inconsistency: Derek Mahon's Verse Letters', *Irish University Review*, Vol. 24, 1, 1994, p. 96.
12 Kelly Sullivan, 'Derek Mahon: Letters to Iceland' in Jefferson Holdridge and Brian Ó Conchubhair (eds), *Post-Ireland?: Essays on Contemporary Irish Poetry* (Wake Forest University Press, 2017), p. 81.
13 Anne Fogarty, 'Foreword' in Robert Brazeau and Derek Gladwin (eds), *Eco-Joyce: The Environmental Imagination of James Joyce* (Cork University Press, 2014), p. xvi.

14 Derek Mahon, 'Out There', *New Collected Poems* (Gallery Press, 2011), p. 163.
15 Derek Mahon, *The Hudson Letter* (Gallery Press, 1995), p. 49.
16 Derek Mahon, *Against the Clock* (Gallery Press, 2018), p. 38.
17 David G. Williams, 'Poet in New York: Derek Mahon's *The Hudson Letter*', *Canadian Journal of Irish Studies,* Vol 23, No 1, July 1997, pp 87–95.
18 Derek Mahon, 'London Time', *New Collected Poems* (Gallery Press, 2011), p. 175.
19 Derek Mahon, 'Beauty and the Beast', *New Collected Poems* p. 185.
20 John Berryman, *The Dream Songs: Poems* (FSG, 1997), p. 334.
21 Derek Mahon, 'Letter from New York: Village Voices' in Terence Brown (ed.) *Journalism: Selected Prose 1970–1995* (Gallery Press, 1996), p. 238.
22 Robert Cowan, 'Introduction and Notes' in John Davie (trans.), *Horace: Satires and Epistles* (Oxford University Press, 2011).
23 Cowan, p. xxi.
24 *Ibid*, p. xiv.
25 *Ibid*, p. 65.
26 *New Collected Poems*, p. 163.
27 Haughton, p. 227.
28 Eamon Grennan, 'Derek Mahon: The Art of Poetry No. 82', *The Paris Review*, Spring 2000, Issue 152, pp 11–12.
29 M.L. Rosenthal, 'Poetry as Confession', *The Nation*, 189 (19 November 1959), pp 154–55.
30 Adam Kirsch, The Wounded Surgeon: Confession and Transformation in Six American Poets (Norton, 2005), p. 1.
31 *Ibid*, p. 2.
32 *Ibid*, p. 104.
33 Grennan, p. 7.
34 Haughton, p. 220.
35 Kirsch, p. 33.
36 *Ibid*, p. 4.
37 *Ibid*, p. 1.
38 Elmer Kennedy-Andrews, 'Derek Mahon: Resident Alien', *Northern Irish Poetry: The American Connection* (Palgrave Macmillan, 2014), p. 115.
39 Grennan, p. 14.
40 Neil Corcoran, '"Resident Alien": The Poetry of Derek Mahon', in Elmer Kennedy-Andrews (ed.), *The Poetry of Derek Mahon* (Colin Smythe, 2002), p. 242.

41 Robert Phillips, *The Confessional Poets* (Southern Illinois University Press, 1973), p. 10.
42 *Ibid*, pp 4–5.
43 *Ibid*, p. 9.
44 Heather Clark, *The Ulster Renaissance: Poetry in Belfast 1962–72* (Oxford University Press, 2006), p. 109.
45 Clark, p. 137.
46 *Ibid*, p. 114.
47 Eileen Simpson, *Poets in Their Youth: A Memoir* (Random House, 1982), p. 253.
48 Kirsch, p. 86.
49 *Ibid*, p. 198.
50 Gillian White, *Lyric Shame: The 'Lyric' Subject of Contemporary American Poetry* (Harvard University Press, 2014), p. 212.
51 *Ibid*, p. 100.
52 *Ibid*. p. 98.
53 Brendan Corcoran, Review of Stephen Enniss, *After the Titanic: A Life of Derek Mahon*, *New Hibernia Review*, Vol. 20, Number 4, Winter 2016, pp 147–52.
54 Redmond, p. 96.
55 White, p. 102.
56 Stephen Enniss, *After the Titanic: A Life of Derek Mahon* (Gill and Macmillan, 2015), pp 222–41.
57 Anthony Cronin, *Dead as Doornails* (Lilliput Press, 1999), pp 187–88.
58 Enniss, p. 225
59 Derek Mahon, 'At Aristaeus' House', *Red Sails* (Gallery Press, 2014), p. 34.
60 Stephanie Brown, *Treating the Alcoholic: A Developmental Model of Recovery* (John Wiley, 1985), p. ix.
61 Enniss, p. 231.
62 Christina Hunt Mahony, 'With Friends Like This …' *Irish Literary Supplement*, Vol. 26, No. 2, Spring 2017, p. 23.
63 *Ibid*.
64 M.G. Stephens, *Where the Sky Ends: A Memoir of Alcohol & Family* (Hazelden, 1999), pp 109–10.
65 Kay Redfield Jamison, *Robert Lowell Setting the River on Fire: A Study of Genius, Mania, and Character* (Knopf, 2017), p. 3.
66 *Ibid*, p. 4.
67 *Ibid*, p. 5.
68 *Ibid*.
69 *Ibid*, p. 9.

70 *Ibid.*
71 *Ibid.*
72 *Ibid*, p. 10.
73 Elizabeth Cook-Lynn, *Why I Can't Read Wallace Stegner and Other Essays: A Tribal Voice* (University of Wisconsin Press, 1996), p. 129.
74 Jim Lucey, *The Life Well Lived: The Therapeutic Journey to Recovery and Wellbeing* (Transworld Ireland, 2017), p. 135.
75 *Ibid*, p. 20.
76 *Ibid*, p. xi.
77 *Ibid*, p. 21.
78 *Ibid.*
79 *Ibid*, pp 8–11.
80 *Ibid*, p. 13.
81 *Ibid*, p. 19.
82 Kirsch, p. 1.
83 André Aciman, 'Temporizing', *Alibis: Essays on Elsewhere* (Picador, 2011), p. 72.
84 E.H. Griffith (et al.), *Alcoholism in the United States: Racial and Ethnic Consideration, Report 181* (American Psychiatric Press, 1986), p. 70.
85 Robert H. and Jeanette C. Lauer, *Social Problems and the Quality of Life* (McGraw-Hill, 2011), p. 45.
86 Kerby Miller, Arnold Schrier, Bruce D. Boling, David N. Doyle (eds), *Irish Immigrants in the Land of Canaan: Letters and Memoirs from Colonial and Revolutionary America, 1675–1815* (Oxford University Press, 2003), p. 9.
87 Peter McDonald, 'History and Poetry: Derek Mahon and Tom Paulin', in Elmer Andrews (ed.) *Contemporary Irish Poetry: A Collection of Critical Essays* (Macmillan, 1992), p. 87.
88 Grennan, p. 10.
89 Edward Said, *Reflections on Exile and Other Essays* (Harvard University Press, 2000), p. xi.
90 *Ibid*, p. xii.
91 *Ibid*, pp 184–85.
92 Haughton, p. 260.
93 Said, p. 186.

REFERENCES

Aciman, André, 'New York, Luminous', *Alibis: Essays on Elsewhere* (Picador, 2011, pp 151–157).
Bellow, Saul, *Humboldt's Gift* (Viking, 1975).

Coleman, Philip, 'On Verse Letters', in Erik Martiny (ed.), *A Companion to Poetic Genre* (Wiley-Blackwell, 2011, pp 505–520).

Costello, Mary. *Academy Street* (Picador, 2016).

Dardis, Tom, *The Thirsty Muse: Alcohol and the American Writer* (Houghton-Mifflin, 1991).

DeLillo, Don, *Underworld* (Scribner, 2003).

Dryden, John, 'Absalom and Achitophel' in Keith Walker ed., *John Dryden: The Major Works* (Oxford University Press, 2003, pp 177–204).

Enright, Anne, *The Green Road* (Norton, 2015).

Gordon, Mary, *Final Payments* (Anchor, 2006).

Hamill, Pete, *A Drinking Life: A Memoir* (Back Bay Books, 1999).

Hamilton, Ian, *Robert Lowell: A Biography* (Random House, 1982).

Kelly, Mary Pat, *Galway Bay* (Grand Central Publishing, 2011).

Johnston, Dillon, *Irish Poetry after Joyce* (University of Notre Dame Press, 1987).

Joyce, James, *Dubliners* (Penguin Classics, 2014).

Kazin, Alfred, *A Walker in the City* (Harvest, 1969).

Kennedy, William, *Ironweed* (Penguin, 1984).

Lewis, Sinclair, *Babbitt* (Bantam Classics, 1998).

Longley, Edna, *Poetry and Posterity* (Bloodaxe Books, 2000).

Lowell, Robert, *Life Studies* (Faber, 1959).

McCann, Colum, *Let the Great World Spin* (Random House, 2008).

McDermott, Alice, *At Weddings and Wakes* (Picador, 2009).
    Charming Billy (FSG, 1999).

McDonagh, Martin, *The Beauty Queen of Leenane & Other Plays* (Vintage, 1998).

Mahon, Derek, *New Selected Poems* (Gallery Press, 2016).
    'Rising Late', *Against the Clock* (Gallery Press, 2018).

Muldoon, Paul, *Moy Sand and Gravel* (FSG, 2002).

O'Hara, Frank, *Standing Still and Walking in New York* (Grey Fox Press, 1981).
    Lunch Poems (City Lights Books, 1964).

O'Neill, Joseph, *Netherland* (Vintage, 2009).

Quinn, Justin, 'Commotions of the Air: A Poet Who Does Not "Sweat the Small Stuff"', *TLS*, 5 January 2018, No. 5988, p. 16.

Quinn, Peter, *The Banished Children of Eve* (Overlook Press, 2008).

Shanley, John Patrick, *Doubt: A Parable* (Theatre Communications, 2005).

Stannard, Martin, *Muriel Spark: The Biography* (Norton, 2010).

Tobin, Daniel, *The Book of Irish American Poetry from the Eighteenth Century to the Present* (University of Notre Dame Press, 2007).

'Scots-Irish Diaspora in Irish American Poetry' in Ferguson, Frank and Richard MacMaster (eds), *Ulster-Scots and America: Diaspora Literature, History, and Migration, 1750–2000* (Four Courts Press, 2016).

Tóibín, Colm, *Brooklyn* (Scribner, 2009).

Jean Valentine in Ireland

At the beginning of William Kennedy's *Ironweed*, set in Albany in 1938, Francis Phelan finds himself 'riding up the winding road of Saint Agnes Cemetery in the back of a rattling old truck'.[1] Self-destructive, down on his luck, prone to violence and an alcoholic, Phelan has found temporary employment as a day labourer shovelling dirt in the graveyard. While at work, he engages in wishful conversations with his own deceased family members who are interred there and takes comfort from the sense of order that the cemetery pervades. He observes how the interred Irish have been grouped together, for the most part, and even how Saint Agnes' arrangers have reaffirmed social class so that the world of the dead is a mirror image of the one populated by the living:

> 'Look at that tomb,' Francis said to his companion. 'Ain't that somethin'? That's Arthur T. Grogan. I saw him around Albany when I was a kid. He owned all of the electricity in town.'
> 'He ain't got much of it now,' Rudy said.
> 'Don't bet on it,' Francis said. 'Them kind of guys hang on to a good thing.'[2]

Francis Phelan concludes that 'being dead here would situate a man in place and time'.[3] Of course, the sense of order that Phelan discovers is wishful and illusory. Many Irish Americans, for example, have German surnames and will be quick to remind you just where their loyalties lie. Perhaps, such individuals, God forbid, have been misfiled in St Agnes'. The opposite can be equally true with some found interred in the Irish section whose only connection to Irish America is a family name. Irish Americans of Scotch Irish ancestry will not be interred in St Agnes' Cemetery nor will others who were claimed by the great American melting pot be found there – reincarnated into other guises though perhaps still Irish American. Who can tell! For every hundred who claim to be proudly Irish American, there may well be a dozen or so who have used relocation to the United States as opportunities to be freed from their received ethnic, religious and cultural designations. Irish Americans make their way to Ireland to renew ancient ties with the homeland while, at the same time, a smaller group of émigrés travel to the Americas to leave it all behind. For them, Ireland has been given up as a dead loss.

Writing of Irish American poetry in his revised edition of *The Irish Voice in America* in 2000, ten years after the original volume had been published, Charles Fanning observed:

> Two significant shifts in the Irish ethnic literary territory over the decades of the 1990s should be noted here as well. The first is the coming of age of Irish American poetry. For most of its two centuries' existence, the corpus of poetry engaged with the Irish immigrant/ethnic experience has been cursed with the twin afflictions of nostalgia for the old country and polemic about Irish nationalism. There has been in recent years a great sea change here ...[4]

Fanning also points out that 'the new poetic enterprise has also been reinforced by the accelerating cultural interaction between America and Ireland', with many American poets establishing and retaining footholds in Ireland, some permanent.[5] Our sense of how interesting and complex Irish American poetry is has been further deepened by the publication of Daniel Tobin's *The Book of Irish American Poetry from the Eighteenth Century to the Present* in 2007. It is a work that someone with Francis Phelan's more essentialist view of the world would find perplexing, including as it does the work of such poets as Czeslaw Milosz, James Schuyler, Wallace Stevens, Jean Valentine as well as the more familiar gathering of Kellys, Kinsellas, Galvins and Byrnes. On first glance, it might appear that some writers have been simply misfiled. In his introduction, Tobin argues:

> I raise such intractable issues now [ethnicity, tradition, etc], however belatedly and briefly, if only to shift the question of whether there is a tradition of Irish American poetry away from 'generic templates' and clearly identifiable Irish American contexts toward an understanding of tradition that is flexible enough to embrace an inclusiveness and plurality that might keep alive the question of tradition in the ongoing process of seeking to define it. From this perspective, the neglect of explicit Irish American themes in the work of certain prominent Irish American poets becomes an essential part of the story. At the same time, the motifs of travel and exile, often with reference to water, and the recurrent figure of 'the west,' perhaps constitute an almost unconscious subtext for the theme of diaspora in Irish American poetry.[6]

In Tobin's view, F. Scott Fitzgerald's work, largely devoid of an Irish context, is granted an Irish American foothold as is Wallace Stevens' given his imaginative embrace of Ireland, a physical space on which he did not once set foot. Another dynamic at work in recent scholarship is Fanning's sense of a 'new poetic enterprise' and Tobin's revision of this, his reminder that the tradition had always been an energetic one, it is just that we had spent too long looking under the wrong rocks. Tobin's view, for me, is an example of good literary criticism and good citizenship. Inclusivity lends both weight, context and complexity to Irish American poetry. At the same time one can share Fanning's disappointment at, and suspicion of, Fitzgerald's erasure of his upbringing though, for my part, I would argue that the real loss is of his talents – it would have been wonderful to have read his imaginings of Irish America. But Fitzgerald was interested in looking elsewhere, to our benefit, and America in its many proliferations provides many choices. Perhaps when he looked toward his Irish ancestry Fitzgerald found little in the 'twin afflictions of nostalgia for the old country and polemic about Irish nationalism' to engage him.[7] Looking from the present back into the past of Irish American writing requires the dual guidance provided by Fanning's and Tobin's scholarly approaches. Both are indispensable.

At root level, men and women who write are writers first rather than Irish American writers, Catholic writers, Latino/a American writers, and it is often not useful to the author to be burdened with heavy adjectival weight. Likely, Irish American as a hold-all is often more useful to the scholar/reader than to the writer. Also, given the complexity of belonging in a world where movement is so common – life being a journey and the journey being home, to paraphrase Bashō – allegiance to place is often complex and allows for, in my view, multiple and deep attachments to places. Often, we are defined by places rather than by one place. One can be Irish, American, Irish American, while also sharing allegiances to other places – France, Japan, Australia, for example – where one has spent time. To divide an immigrant life into its Irish and American parts can often be erroneous, the man or woman often having spent defining periods of his/her life in another place or places. Equally, the nature of an American's relationship to Ireland can be unusually complicated, even accidental. Jean Valentine came to Ireland to live when she married a man who resided there.

Colm Tóibín spends a large part of each year in the US though few consider him to be American or even Irish American.

In 1986, the American author and environmentalist Rebecca Solnit became an Irish citizen as the beneficiary of family genealogical fieldwork and the account she provides of her relationship to Ireland is one that is shared by many American writers who have gained a foothold in Ireland:

> On the last day of 1986, I became an Irish citizen. My newfound status as a European has not yet ceased to amuse me – my purple passport with its golden harp seems less like a birthright than a slim book on the mythologies of blood, heritage, and emigration ... I hasten to disclaim any great authority on the subjects of Irish history and culture ... This is likewise no core sample of contemporary Ireland; in the same spirit Irish tourists may head straight for Graceland, I took off for the places that appealed to me and let attraction and invitations stitch together the rest of my route ... In other terms, this excursion offered me a whole set of linked possibilities: to muse about the identity politics raised by my American activism and my Irish passport; to rethink my education in English literature ...[8]

In *A Book of Migrations*, a meditation on her travels in Ireland, Solnit allows the road ahead to serve as her guide with the result that she absorbs Irish thought, topography and belonging, both from the physical locations she has chosen to visit and from engagements forged by accidental encounters with individuals. Unlike visitors who travel with a narrower purpose – a business executive on a visit to a town where his company seeks to acquire a competitor, or a couple intent on finding family roots in a rural townland – Solnit seeks to walk among the Irish in their home places. She hopes to understand something of herself and her connection to Ireland, to stand at the intersections where bodies and histories collide. At no time does she wish to claim ownership of Irish space, whether physical, psychological or literary. His life perspective changed by serious illness, Patrick Kavanagh wrote in the preface to his *Collected Poems* that he had lost his 'messianic compulsion. My purpose in life was to have no purpose', and this mantra guided his work's last phase.[9] In a similar vein, American writers like Solnit arrive in Ireland with no greater purpose than to simply be in place on an island that has caught their attention, or they have been drawn to accidently. For those lacking Irish ancestry, Ireland can be an idea, a longing, or both. It is frequently through reading Irish books or listening to Irish music that people become drawn towards Ireland – both can transcend inherited pasts.

Before Valentine's arrival, many other American poets had spent time in Ireland – Robert Lowell, John Berryman and Muriel Rukeyser are three examples – while others settled there: Knute Skinner, Anne Kennedy and Julie O'Callaghan being three among many. Richard Tillinghast, like Valentine a poet who took part in Lowell's poetry workshops in Harvard, has spent a great deal of time living and writing in Ireland. Other poets are equally at home and resident in both countries: Eamon Grennan in Upstate New York and Galway; Tess Gallagher in the Pacific Northwest and Co. Sligo. Writing of American poets who have become resident in Ireland, Daniel Tobin argues that being in Ireland can hinder growth in readership in the US:

> while a growing number of Irish American poets have spent a significant amount of time in Ireland, with some moving there permanently, the countercrossing back to Ireland does not carry the same urgency or potential for acknowledgment in the United States. Going over there will not necessarily increase a poet's visibility to an American readership.[10]

Travelling in the opposite direction, many Irish poets – Seamus Heaney, Paul Muldoon, Eavan Boland – have seen their visibility and readership increase as a result of their presence in the US. Just as Muldoon, Boland and other Irish poets who live in the US retain homes, footholds and identifications in Ireland, Jean Valentine retained her New York apartment while in Sligo and continued to publish widely in the US while also submitting her work to such Irish journals as *Cyphers*, *Cúirt Journal* and *Poetry Ireland Review*. The lives and allegiances of contemporary writers complicate notions of home, nationality and belonging.

Jean Valentine, who was born in Chicago in 1934, spent most of her childhood in Massachusetts where she was educated at Milton Academy Girls' School and Radcliffe College from which she graduated in 1956 with a degree in English. In 1964 a collection of her poetry was awarded the Yale Series of Younger Poets Award and was published in 1965 as *Dream Barker and Other Poems*. For *Door in the Mountain: New and Collected Poems 1965–2003*, Valentine received the National Book Award. As a result of her relationship with and subsequent marriage to the artist Barrie Cooke, Valentine lived in Ireland from 1989–1996, principally in Kilmactranny, near Lough Arrow, in Co. Sligo. Valentine and Cooke had known each other decades before when both were students in the Boston area. Here, I will explore work in *The River at Wolf* (1992), *Growing Darkness, Growing Light* (1997), and *The Cradle of the Real Life* (2000), the collections that include Valentine's Irish poems. In addition to being guided by Charles Fanning, Daniel Tobin and Rebecca Solnit, I will also make use of materials gathered from a visit to the Schlesinger Library at Radcliffe/Harvard where Jean Valentine's papers are housed. The papers present in this archive, her correspondence and biographical information in particular, provide useful insights into the literary aspect of her life in Ireland. Valentine's Irish correspondents included Seamus Heaney, Dennis O'Driscoll, Cathal Ó Searcaigh, Paula Meehan, Peter Fallon and Nuala Ní Dhomhnaill. An experienced leader of poetry workshops at American universities, Valentine taught creative writing courses for Kilkenny VEC in 1991–1992 and 1993–1994 where her students were drawn from the local community rather than from the college campus. In this respect, her efforts complement Eavan Boland's pioneering work in this regard; in particular, these workshops provided opportunities for women poets to engage with audiences for the first time. The Radcliffe archive includes a letter from Prionsias Ó Drisceoil, arts education organiser for the south east, praising Valentine for her great efforts on behalf of her students and for the quality of her teaching. Clearly Valentine's level of engagement in the Irish literary enterprise is reflective of the resident rather than of the tourist. Her commitment is expressed in 'He Says to Me, In Ireland':

> But I want those women's lives
> rage   constraints
> the poems they burned
> in their chimney-throats
> The History
> of the World Without Words
> more than your silver or your gold art.[11]

For Valentine, the lives and histories of Irish women must emerge from silence to be heard and be given precedence over the accessories, such as torcs, that were forged for women to wear and be defined by.

Salmon published *The Under Voice*, a volume of Valentine's selected poems in 1995. For both *The Under Voice* and *Growing Darkness, Growing Light* (1997), Valentine acknowledges the Tyrone Guthrie Centre at Annamakerrig where she wrote and revised poems and added the poignant note to the latter, 'I owe a special debt of thanks to all who have offered me so much literary hospitality in Ireland'.[12] Barrie Cooke provided the author's photo and cover art for *Growing Darkness, Growing Light*. By the time this book was published, Valentine's

Irish life had ended: she had retreated home to New York. 'November', from *The Cradle of the Real Life* (2000) is perhaps both a re-stating of the incompatibilities dividing men from women, Ireland from America, the surface from the inner life, body from soul, as well as being a gorgeous song of departure from Ireland, simultaneously broken-hearted and coldly objective:

> November
> leaving Ireland
>
> Sligo Bay and the two mountains
> the female and the male
> walking down the stairs
> into the ground
>
> – I have to leave
> And I have to watch.[13]

Ben Bulben is the man, and Knocknarae the woman. The first W.B. Yeats, the second Queen Meadhbh. The first, Barrie Cooke, the second Jean Valentine. Ireland is the woman.

One way to gauge Jean Valentine's response to Ireland is to catalogue her Irish poems, though this is a fraught endeavour given that her work is never reliably fixed in place or theme and weaves its path casually through conscious and subconscious spaces. Of the fifty-six poems in *The River at Wolf* (1992), two, perhaps, have Irish settings; ten of forty-three in *Growing Darkness, Growing Light* (1997); and of the forty-six in *The Cradle of the Real Life* (2000) four can be identified as being connected to Ireland. In Ireland, Valentine retained her American interests and sensibility – the formal shapes and recurring themes present in her poems reflect continuity as she takes part in 'a pilgrimage toward the parts of ourselves that are lost and found'.[14] Unconnected to Ireland before her arrival, she did not seek to wholly remake herself on settling in. In fact, to a woman accustomed to New York, the area around Lough Arrow in Co. Sligo might have seemed rather backward and quiet. Valentine's work is built on inscape, dreams, mythology, palimpsest, and, as Michael Waters has noted, Valentine is like Raymond Carver 'a master of limited vocabulary';[15] she eschews traditional narrative, 'her poems don't speak *about*; for the most part they speak *to*' with the result that tying down meaning and location can be difficult.[16] She is 'committed to interiority'.[17] For Kathleen Fagley:

> Valentine's lifework is listening; listening dominates the spare poems in her last four books: *The River at Wolf, Growing Darkness, Growing Light, The Cradle of the Real Life,* and *Door in the Mountain.*[18]

As readers we listen though the beautiful images that form these poems come from afar and are heard as distant echoes. Unlike many poets, as Kazim Ali shows us, 'Valentine herself does not have an accompanying critical work or poetics statements that enable us to accurately track her aesthetic commitments'.[19] In this respect, her career is reminiscent of Eiléan Ní Chuilleanáin's, a contemporary Irish poet who also does not provide a body of prose to accompany her poetry. It is problematic to attach Valentine's poetry too closely to Ireland: though she wrote little about Ireland when she returned to the US, American themes dominate work written in Ireland. Given the interiority at the heart of her poetry, tracing Valentine's topography is a fraught activity. And, she is not a poet of place as we understand it in the Irish context.

In the years before coming to Ireland, Valentine made two decisions that radically changed her ways of thinking about living and writing: her conversion to Catholicism and her decision to give up drinking:

> I feel that all poetry is prayer, it's just as simple as that. Who else would we be talking to? I think the intensity in a poem may be because it is so prayerful – it's intense in the way that a song is, but in a way that prose isn't, and doesn't attempt to be … I think that now more than ten years ago, and being sober,

not drinking, I can acknowledge rage. I can acknowledge violence – a lot of things that were intellectually clear to me, but that I couldn't in my stomach acknowledge before.[20]

Interesting enough, she arrived in Ireland at a time when many people had begun to turn away from Catholicism and when the literary drinking culture of Kavanagh and Behan had largely passed into myth. She would have noticed the burgeoning presence of women poets in Ireland and known about the controversy surrounding the exclusion of women from *The Field Day Anthology of Irish Writing* (1992).

Writing on *The River at Wolf* (1992), Valentine's first volume containing Irish themes, Martha Collins notes the important place this book claims in her development:

> The most self-contained of her collections, it also looks back to earlier volumes, especially the first, *Dream Barker* (1965), which can be read as a kind of urtext for it. The place of *The River at Wolf* in Valentine's career is important: the first book to appear after the new and selected *Home Deep Blue* (1989), it was also Valentine's first full-length collection since 1979.[21]

It is clear that Valentine arrived in Ireland at a key point in her life as a writer – a convert, sober and ready to embark on the next part of her life as lover and writer. This updraft is given eloquent voice in the title poem:

> This close to God this close to you:
> walking into the river at Wolf with
> the animals. The snake's
> green skin, lit from inside. Our second life.[22]

Jeffrey Skinner sees this poem as having an:

> Irish manner; powerful understatement blended with factual acceptance of the supernatural ... Very un-American, in a way – especially Jean's casual, unironic use of the word *God*. Almost as if she had not been paying close attention to the literary magazines for the past thirty or so years.[23]

Perhaps the manner of *The River at Wolf* is less Irish than Catholic though Skinner's illustration of Valentine's going against the grain holds weight. With regard to her conversion to Catholicism, Valentine belongs with Evelyn Waugh, Graham Greene and Muriel Spark rather than with Ireland's born, bred and resistant Irish Catholic writers. Even her teacher Robert Lowell was a Catholic for a significant period. Two powerful responses in Valentine's work of this time are to the devastation caused by AIDS and to her mother's death – work shaded and informed, we might imagine, by Valentine's presence in Ireland. *The River at Wolf* also contains poems on Western American landscapes, work written, perhaps, from an imagination that had absorbed something of the *dinnseanchas* of County Sligo. Unless specifically engaged in the practice of travel writing, writers need not be fully focused on their present locations with the personal (the loss of a mother) and the place where the personal and public engage (the AIDS epidemic) of interest and importance across boundaries. Even in the collection's most Irish poem, 'Barrie's Dream, the Wild Geese', expectation is undercut by allusion when a Robert Lowell conversation is interrupted by the geese:

> The sound of their wings!
> Oars rowing, laborious, wood against wood: it was
> a continuing thought, no, it was a labor,
> how to accept your lover's love. Who could do it alone?
> Under our radiant sleep they were bearing us all night long.[24]

The rowers might be on the Charles or East River or even on Lough Arrow – it is impossible to tell and unnecessary to know given that this is a dream poem. Valentine has said that 'I owe more to the poem than the audience', with the result we can frequently be blindsided by her work's manoeuvrings.[25] The lovers in the poem are supported by the great friends: Elizabeth Bishop and Robert Lowell.

In her review of *Growing Darkness, Growing Light* (1997) for *The Nation*, Carol Muske Dukes made particular note of Valentine's use of listening and dreams:

> The precise language of consciousness is dramatized by Valentine's 'listening' technique. Poetry exalts the interchangeable worlds of dimness where 'growing' darkness and light blur the distinction between external and internal ... The poems in this book are indeed dreams, but precise dreams of waking: startling junctures of the abstract and the carnal.[26]

Though Valentine touches on the thematic staples that underline American representations of Ireland, her Irish verse can be quiet, cryptic and Celanesque. However, in *Growing Darkness, Growing Light* she engages with narrative, the engine that drives much of Irish poetry, though in Valentine's hands it is subverted and knotted. In 'Long Irish Summer Day', the familiar, rural and stable is undermined as the poem's visual field narrows from the exterior to the inner:

> A lorry scatters
> hay down the road
> red as blood.
>
> Down by Tommy Flynn's
> a young man is sowing
> in the ten o'clock sunset
>
> sowing salt tears on the road
> – not for the ice, we already have sand.
>
> Sun and moon shine into our glass room,
> two countries, two cities,
> two glass houses:
> a shotgun is hanging on the wall.[27]

It is a poem of binaries working at cross-purposes as increasing divisions open as the poem develops through its stanzas – from reaping and sowing to the glass room where under sun and moon the binaries appear most visceral. The 'shotgun hanging on the wall' brings to mind Moran's weapon and his ever-present threats of violence in John McGahern's *Amongst Women*, a well-known contemporary novel of the region of Ireland where Valentine resided. One moving and tender aspect of her marriage is provided by a sequence near the end of *Growing Darkness, Growing Light* treating of Barrie Cooke's hospitalisation in Dublin as a result of a heart attack:

> The surgeon said,
> 'You don't have to visit,
> he won't remember it.
> Ten minute visits.'
>
> Everyone here walks in a deep
> open-eyed and rigid sleep.
> In this deep
> black unfold
>
> we don't know what is happening to us,
> no more than the dumb beasts of the field ...[28]

Often in Valentine's dreamscapes, matters that are unfocused develop clarity; however, in the hospital, an institution devoted to healing, human beings are reduced to purely animal states. In 'The Tractors', Valentine, the deep-seeing outsider, renders the family and comforting rural scene as something heavy and frightful:

> The tractors at night,
> the dimly-lighted
> kindly lobsters
> with glass sides,
> with men inside,
> and at home, wives,
> and depression's black dogs
> walking out of
> the January hedges'
> hacked-off sides.[29]

In this one sentence single breath poem Valentine makes a violent dispatch of the rural sublime. The ubiquitous tractor is both monstrous and comforting-looking; it is where the men are housed with work divided – again her vision is underlined by binaries – between the duties allotted to men and women, Valentine reading rural Ireland in like manner to Alice Munro's reading of rural Ontario. Rather than providing uplift, rural Ireland in winter puts people on the road to depression. Great measures of hope and possibility have been 'hacked-off' like the limbs of the hedges running along the roadsides.

In a letter of 26 April 2000 to Valentine, following the publication of *The Cradle of the Real Life*, Dennis O'Driscoll wondered:

> Is it a desperate need on my part to claim a bit of you for Irish poetry that makes me feel that your years among us have brought your work to a new level of freshness and intensity?[30]

Given the trajectory of Valentine's career, this is a quite a perceptive statement echoing what Martha Collins has written in her overview of Valentine's career. Following early success, Valentine's visibility dimmed in the 1970s, in no small measure as a result of her being dropped by her New York publisher. Although she continued to publish books and her work appeared in the most visible outlets, such as *The New Yorker*, her books were overlooked. *The Cradle of the Real Life*, her first book for Wesleyan University Press, received extensive notice and was followed by *Door in the Mountain: New and Collected Poems 1965–2003*, winner of the National Book Award. Clearly, Wesleyan had a sense of Valentine's value as a poet and an expertise to properly market her books: both collections were extensively and favourably reviewed. Also, the first section of *Door in the Mountain* is quite magnificent, her strongest work to date. In the Irish American context, we should heed O'Driscoll's counsel and think of Valentine's years in Ireland as a period of gestation. She was writing great poems and preparing to write even better ones. Her time in Ireland provided Valentine with a new space in which to think and write; she was newly-married and in rural Ireland freed from her complex New York connections. She could look to the future with nothing to lose. Ireland nurtured her.

The Cradle of the Real Life is rich, harrowing and deeply moving. Exploring the second half of this collection, where many Irish-themed poems are located, Amy Newman notes that it is a gathering of poems of:

> interiors, separations, little exiles, incompletion. The sequence is classic in its contrast and simultaneity: porous and hidden, pervious and allusive, demanding and welcoming, like a transom, like a lighted window ... Attending these divisions are implied, imperceptible attachments – invisible lines, like radio signals, between the entities.[31]

Lee Upton sees Valentine as 'a poet of departures'.[32] In the 'Her Lost Book' sequence, Valentine gathers up aspects of her own life so that the work is, in part, a richly allusive, minimalist autobiography in verse, though one where the poet is very firmly aware of the lives lived by other women whose stories inform her own. One senses dissolution from the first section of *The Cradle of the Real Life*: of Valentine's marriage, the death of friends such as Jane Kenyon and others who are eulogised or alluded to, including her parents. But dissolution leads to a re-affirmation of Valentine's commitment to writing because it is where what has occurred might be understood:

> I ask for a dream
> about my marriage:
> 'Ink.' Ink. Ink. Ink.
>
> My ink-stained hand
> his paint-smudged hand.[33]

In 'The Pen', the book's first poem, Valentine responds to and revises the ideas explored by Seamus Heaney in 'Digging', the first poem in *Death of a Naturalist*, with the focus here on 'thought' rather than on the more active imperative that Heaney proposes. Both Heaney's and Valentine's poems are rooted in Virgil's *Georgics* where these tropes were originally formulated.

'Her Lost Book', the second section of *The Cradle of the Real Life*, is divided into three parts: with the exception of 'He Says to Me, in Ireland', all of the poems refer to the lives of other women, as individuals and as parts of collectives.

Near the end of the first part is 'Reading the Mandelstams' a lyric that evokes another marriage of artists and, like Valentine's project here, is a union recalled by a woman/wife. Part two is a recording of many of the more painful aspects of Valentine's own life: family difficulties, alcoholism, mental health issues and hospitalisation, single parenthood and undergoing an abortion procedure as a consequence of poverty:

> I thought:
> You live somewhere
> deeper than the well
> I live down in.
> Deeper than anything from me or him.
>
> No but it took me
> time to see you, thirty earth years.[34]

Individual poems often reprise themes already explored throughout Valentine's career, though here they are formed into a single group as the poet makes an inventory of her life. As Lee Upton points out:

> autobiography is rendered problematic by her enactments of psychological fusion between individuals and by her rendering of personalities that are more permeable in her work than conventional autobiography allows.[35]

The third section comprises two poems, 'To Ireland' and 'Home', with both divided into sections. It is possible that all of this part can be regarded as being Irish or sharing an Irish starting point; at the same time, given the deep well that Valentine draws from, one can never be certain. As I have mentioned already, the place of Valentine's poetry is not the traditional topographic place favoured by Irish poets, Medbh McGuckian being an exception. This sequence's final part is not intended to provide synthesis. On the level of diction and allusion, Valentine appears to be making a strong embrace of Joyce as she winds towards the end of her Irish journey: snow is falling, a river is named, water is important, a person is looking out of a window, night has fallen, a marriage is broken (all calling to mind the closing scenes of *The Dead*), and the use of 'Home' as an ironic title recalls Stephen's use of the same word in his conversation with the English dean in *Portrait*. There is no resolution for Valentine so she must, like Joyce, leave. James Joyce left Ireland to go into exile whereas Jean Valentine left Sligo to go home to New York. One feels in these poems, however, Valentine's deep sense of loss for her Irish world. The sequence ends with two important gestures, calling to mind the end of Eavan Boland's 'Anna Liffey', another work of revision: the first of these is reaffirmation of the woman as poet:

> Snow
> falling slow
> filling our footprints
>
> writing a word
> changing it
>
> night
> at the window
> two birches, blown together.[36]

and the second of a woman alive in the world:

> Snow falling
> off the Atlantic
>
> out toward strangeness
>
> you
> a breath on a coal[37]

For Valentine, home is the page. Home is the body. The quotation from St Mechtilde of Magdeburg that Valentine provides to conclude part one of *The Cradle of the Real Life* provides the religious context to her idea of projective breath and underlines how deeply Catholicism guides the poet:

> Do not fear your death, for when it arrives I will draw my breath and your soul will come to me like a needle to a magnet[38]

One might add that the voice is the medium of the soul. Hear the voice. Read the poem. Reveal the soul.

To label Jean Valentine as an Irish American or Irish poet makes sense if one follows Charles Fanning's and Daniel Tobin's separate modes of linking poets to both Ireland and its diaspora. Though not of Irish background, Valentine lived in Ireland, was engaged in the literary world as a founder of the Scríobh Literary Festival in Sligo with Leland Bardwell, Dermot Healy and others and served as a facilitator of community poetry workshops. Ireland is a vivid, if understated, presence in her work. Jean Valentine has left enduring marks on the literary map of Ireland. But to believe that she is an Irish American and/or Irish poet is to eliminate what most scholars would consider the fuller facts of Valentine's American life and literary achievement. In *Jean Valentine: This-World Company*, a collection of essays recounting her career as an author, only passing references are devoted to her Irish life, though over time, as readers learn more about her experiences there, this may change. Many of the contributors to the volume of essays highlight Valentine's sense of literary kinship with Mandelstam, Celan, Rilke and Borges indicating that her work is best understood outside of a strict national or ethnic context, even ones, like the Irish American or Irish, to which she belongs only tangentially. Poetry is often rooted in place; however, places cannot simply be seen or limited to nations and national literatures because they might more likely be local and international: New York and Kilkenny or New York and Sligo or America and Kilkenny or America and Sligo in Valentine's case. As her correspondence reveals, she established kinship in Ireland with Dennis O'Driscoll, a poet whose work is also local and global: he is of Thurles and Dublin but also of Prague and Kraków. No wonder that O'Driscoll and Valentine developed a friendship.

From her Irish journey, Rebecca Solnit learned much about her relationships to places and about being in motion between them:

> There's a conventional fiction preserved in travel literature, if nowhere else, that a person is wholly in one place at one time. The idea of nativeness is similarly a myth of singularity or perhaps an ideal of it, but even most contemporary more-or-less indigenous people have mixed ancestry, have undergone sudden and violent relocations, have lost something of their past in the process and picked up a lot from the dominant culture of the US, which is itself a hybrid with many sources, not all of them European. We are often in two places at once. In fact, we are usually in at least two places, and occasionally the contrast is evident. I always seem to be trailing through three or four at once: talking about Utah and thinking about Idaho caves while watching a movie about British prisons in an airplane over what was probably Newfoundland on the way to Ireland was nothing exceptional.[39]

Though it is redundant to say so, writing is an imaginative enterprise that draws from multiple parts of the conscious and subconscious. The psyche is not always subject to rational cartography and we do not know what space the author occupies and from what combination exactly she is drawing on at the moment of composition or revision. At a later stage, a book jacket or journal contributor's note will draw our attention – American, Irish, German. Like Solnit and Valentine, many writers are widely formed, bound and of multiple allegiances. At the same time, the literary is bound by its own spaces – pages, bindings, covers – that can conceal as much as they reveal. Neither Rebecca Solnit nor Jean Valentine are conventional and this, at least in part, underlines what makes their works so notable and heralded. Regarding Jean Valentine, we can make too much of her time in Ireland and her Irish work; however, it would be erroneous to ignore it.

Notes

1. William Kennedy, *Ironweed* (Penguin, 1994), p. 1.
2. *Ibid*, p. 2.
3. *Ibid*, p. 13.
4. Charles Fanning, *The Irish Voice in America: 250 Years of Irish American Fiction* (University Press of Kentucky, 2000, 2nd ed.), pp 368–69.
5. *Ibid*, p. 369.
6. Daniel Tobin (ed.), *The Book of Irish American Poetry from the Eighteenth Century to the Present* (University of Notre Dame Press, 2007), p. xiv.
7. Fanning, pp 368–69.
8. Rebecca Solnit, *A Book of Migrations* (Verso, 2011, revised ed.), pp xi–xii.
9. Patrick Kavanagh, *Collected Poems* (Martin Brian & O'Keeffe, 1964), p. xiv.
10. Daniel Tobin, *Awake in America: On Irish American Poetry* (University of Notre Dame Press, 2011), p. 328.
11. Jean Valentine, *Door in the Mountain: New and Collected Poems 1965–2003* (Wesleyan University Press, 2004), p. 266.
12. Jean Valentine, *Growing Darkness, Growing Light* (Carnegie Mellon University Press, 1997).
13. 'November', *Door in the Mountain*, p. 252.
14. Dorothy Barresi, 'Lost and Found: Jean Valentine's Poems of Childhood and Motherhood' in Kazim Ali and John Hoppenthaler (eds), *Jean Valentine: This-World Company* (University of Michigan Press, 2012), p. 87.
15. Michael Waters, '"Through Such Hard Wind and Light": Jean Valentine's Elegy for Elizabeth Bishop' in Kazim Ali and John Hoppenthaler (eds), *Jean Valentine: This-World Company* (University of Michigan Press, 2012, pp 70–4), p. 71.
16. Catherine Barnett, 'Little Light on the Road: An Informal Primer on Reading Jean Valentine, in Six Brief Sections' in Kazim Ali and John Hoppenthaler (eds), *Jean Valentine: This-World Company* (University of Michigan Press, 2012), p. 14.
17. Mark Doty, 'Ghost Sonnets' in Kazim Ali and John Hoppenthaler (eds), *Jean Valentine: This-World Company* (University of Michigan Press, 2012), p. 104.
18. Kathleen Fagley, 'Orpheus and Eurydice and Gestures of Turning: Palimpsest in the Poetry of Jean Valentine' in Kazim Ali and John Hoppenthaler (eds), *Ibid*, p. 56.

19 Kazim Ali, 'Introduction' in Kazim Ali and John Hoppenthaler (eds), *Jean Valentine: This-World Company* (University of Michigan Press, 2012), p. 3.
20 Michael Klein, 'Jean Valentine: An Interview', *American Poetry Review*. Vol. 20, 4, July/August, 1991, pp 39–40.
21 Martha Collins, 'Lit from Inside: Jean Valentine's River at Wolf' in Kazim Ali and John Hoppenthaler (eds), *Jean Valentine: This-World Company* (University of Michigan Press, 2012), p. 92.
22 *Door in the Mountain*, p. 197.
23 Jeffrey Skinner, 'Everyone was Drunk: Reading Jean Valentine through a Shot Glass Lens' in Kazim Ali and John Hoppenthaler (eds), *Ibid*, p. 151.
24 *Door in the Mountain*, p. 198.
25 Celia Bland, 'Talking about Poetry with Jean Valentine', *Washington Review*, Vol. XV, No. 6, April/May, 1990, p. 20.
26 Carol Muske Dukes, 'Time into Language', *The Nation*, 21 July 1997, p. 37.
27 *Door in the Mountain*, pp 229–30.
28 'Open Heart', *Door in the Mountain*, pp 242–3.
29 *Door in the Mountain*, pp 221–2.
30 Dennis O'Driscoll, Papers of Jean Valentine, 1952–2004, Series II: Correspondence (Radcliffe Institute for Advanced Study, Harvard University), 2.1.
31 Amy Newman, '"This Close to God this Close to You": Incarnation in Jean Valentine' in Kazim Ali and John Hoppenthaler (eds), *Jean Valentine: This-World Company* (University of Michigan Press, 2012), p. 127.
32 Lee Upton, *The Muse of Abandonment: Origin, Identity, Mastery in Five American Poets* (Bucknell University Press, 1998), p. 77.
33 'They lead me', *Door in the Mountain*, p. 249.
34 'Abortion Child', *Door in the Mountain*, p. 272.
35 Upton, p. 17.
36 'Home', *Door in the Mountain*, pp 274–75.
37 'Home', *Door in the Mountain*, p. 275.
38 *Door in the Mountain*, pp 266–67.
39 Solnit, p. 9.

REFERENCES

Ali, Kazim and John Hoppenthaler (eds), *Jean Valentine: This-World Company* (University of Michigan Press, 2012).
Boland, Eavan, 'Anna Liffey', *In a Time of Violence* (Norton, 1994).

Deane, Seamus (ed.), *Field Day Anthology of Irish Writing* (Norton, 1992).
Joyce, James, *Dubliners* (Oxford, 2000).
A Portrait of the Artist as a Young Man (Norton, 2007).
McGahern, John, *Amongst Women* (Faber, 1990).
Valentine, Jean, *The Cradle of the Real Life* (Wesleyan University Press, 2000).
The River at Wolf (Alice James Books, 1992).

IRISH AMERICAN FABLES OF RESISTANCE

Writing on Eiléan Ní Chuilleanáin's poetry, Andrew J. Auge highlights the recent change that has taken place in the reputation and role of the Irish Catholic Church, 'by the turn of the millennium, the once imposing edifice of Irish Catholicism appeared increasingly derelict'.[1] Given all we have learned from reports into how the church has dealt with abuses committed by its clergy and cover-ups initiated by its hierarchy, it seems quite fitting that a once proud edifice and standard bearer would appear increasingly derelict. No longer is Sunday Mass the centrepiece of the Irish week; instead, many Catholics flock to shopping centres and malls. In elegantly-lined and nicely-marbled halls, shop assistants pass credit card receipts to consumers while in old cathedrals and cold churches priests look forlornly across the pews and know how easy nowadays it is to count the number of worshipers who will receive communion. Auge, like many Irish American writers and scholars in recent decades, provides timely and nuanced explorations into the role and influence that the Catholic Church has played, and continues to play, in Irish life. Looking toward Ireland from the US, Irish American

Catholic intellectuals, guided by their own traditional upbringings and by American notions of egalitarianism and individual freedom, help us see the past and imagine the future of Irish Catholicism more clearly.

Because of the Church's horrific acts and reluctance to admit wrongdoing, its insistence on moving priests from parish to parish to hide abuses, its refusal to listen to distraught parents, its arrogant disregard for the law, many Irish Catholics have turned their backs on the institution so that the church has now become a ceremonial rather than a vital entity in Irish life. Nevertheless, the Catholic Church is still possessed of elegant rituals and structures and these continue to give formal shape to baptisms, weddings and funerals – many of the key events in people's lives. Even if the church has lost its place in the hearts of many Irish people, it has retained through its elaborate ceremonies much of its symbolic power. Perhaps more than symbols, these solemn rites continue to serve as the meeting places of body and soul, reality and imagination, our lives on earth and in the great beyond. Even at a moment in history when the church has lost its appeal, its cultural legacy retains much that is potent and important, even to its sharpest critics.

In a wonderful essay, 'Getting Here from There: A Writer's Reflections on a Religious Past', Mary Gordon, whose first novel *Final Payments* infuriated traditional American Catholics when it appeared in 1978, reflects on the many-sided role that her Catholic upbringing played in her formation as woman and writer:

> Those names come very easily to my mind – names learned in childhood, memorized in childhood. They form one of those lists, those catalogues that made the blood race with the buildup. So many catalogues there were in the church I grew up in, so many lists: seven capital sins, three theological virtues and four moral ones, seven sacraments, seven gifts of the Holy Ghost. A kind of poetry of accumulation, gaining power like an avalanche from its own momentum.[2]

In addition to paths to faith and integration into a community, the church provided systems and a phenomenology that gave substance to Gordon's world, 'a poetry of accumulation' that would serve as a starting and testing point for her life as an adult. Two important aspects of her cultural upbringing that Gordon highlights are the global and the local and their interplay:

> So to be a Catholic, or even to have been one, is to feel a certain access to a world wider than the vision allowed by the lens of one's own birth. You grew up believing that the parish is the world, and that anyone in the world could be a member of the parish. But of course the parish was a fiercely limited terrain: the perfect size and conformation for the study of the future novelist.[3]

Part of the church's cultural legacy, locally and globally, is a doctrine of inclusiveness, though this has been tempered, as Gordon is quick to point out, by exclusion as a consequence of social class and gender, among other factors. The rooting of the church in the small unit of the parish, and vice versa, indicates the degree to which the church has remained true to Irish and Irish American attachments to and feelings for townland, village, town and city neighbourhood. In this scenario, the relationship between church and worshiper is organic. Also, as Gordon believes, the church's international aspect provides its faithful with contact to a wider world. At some level, the ideal version of the church is a local and global one rather than a national one. It would hardly be an exaggeration to claim that part of the church's legacy is the invention of community itself.

Ultimately, Gordon finds for herself everything that is attractive and honourable in the church to be deposited in individuals and groups and these direct us to the deepest legacy of Catholicism – people who profess to be Catholics:

> I'm in a queer position: the Church of my childhood, which was so important for my formation as an artist, is now gone.

As Gertrude Stein said of Oakland, 'There is no there there.' But there *is* something there, something that formed me and that touches me still: the example of the nuns killed in El Salvador, of liberation theologians standing up to the Pope, of the nuns – the 'Vatican 24' – who signed the statement asserting that it was possible for Catholics to have different positions on abortion and still be Catholics. These sisters, many of them in their sixties and seventies, faced the loss of everything – their sisterhood, their community, their lives, and things we wouldn't think of, like their medical insurance. They had no Social Security; they had no pension plans; they faced literally being thrown out on the street. They are extraordinary women.[4]

There are at least two important elements in this discussion. First, that the church through its theology and individual and collective action by its believers has for long preached the importance of resistance to injustice. As Gordon points out, this injunction continues to be taken seriously by Catholics, even when it entails resistance to the church itself. Rev Liam Ryan, an Irish priest, has noted that the hierarchy should pay close attention to such resistance from women noting that 'male geriatric dictatorship may well have been what finally toppled Communism in Eastern Europe'.[5]

A second element is the role that women have played and continue to play in the church and their embrace of the faith. Women serving as nuns, Mary Gordon and others have pointed out, have played the roles of carers, teachers, doctors and nurses, and they have often been fearless leaders. Gordon reminds us that a church that welcomes everyone does not treat everyone with equality. Implicit in her argument is the positive legacy of nuns that should be widely imitated so that the church can retain something of its soul. As a woman, and an author, and an individual from an Irish American background, Gordon has been quick to speak out and her voice is an influential one. She writes that 'the Catholic Church in America is the Irish Church. And the Irish Church is a church that is obsessed and committed to the idea of keeping silence' and that while the Irish will love to talk to you, they 'don't like to tell you anything'.[6] Today, many brave people who suffered terrible abuse have spoken out and bravely resisted silence. John McGahern took a similar route in 1965 when he published *The Dark* and was driven from his job as a teacher for being so honest. But, to speak out belongs, at least in part, to Catholicism's cultural legacy.

In Ireland, Catholic religious practices incorporate belief systems derived from two traditions – the pre-Christian and the Christian – so to dismiss them would be to invent a specious reality. Also, in both the United States and Ireland, the drift of worshippers away from the church predates the reporting of abuse and had been a consequence of the church's resistance to modernisation and the voices of its flock, as Fr Andrew Greeley has noted of the United States:

> The impression from the outside is that a splendid and sanguine American Catholic Church started hemorrhaging in the 1960s and had yet to stanch its bleeding. Attendance at Mass has fallen off dramatically among practicing Catholics, including some nuns who are dissatisfied enough with the pastorate that they conduct their own Eucharistic services. Catholics live together before marriage and receive the Eucharist – a mortal sin compounded by a sacrilege, according to Baltimore Catechism standards. Nine out of ten reject the Church's position on artificial birth control; Catholics' attitudes on abortion are indistinguishable from those of Protestants. A majority disagree with Vatican teaching on divorce, clerical celibacy, the ordination of women, homosexuality, and the role of the laity – and 80 percent of those see no conflict ignoring Church teaching and being good Catholics ...[7]

Interviewed by Maureen Dezell, Monsignor Kelly of Sacred Heart Parish in Roslindale, Mass., put it another way, 'men got back from the war, they went to college', and:

by the sixties and seventies, priests and nuns who'd once had a free hand were now preaching to people who were as educated as they were if not more so.[8]

In *The Irish Americans: The Rise to Money and Power*, Fr Andrew M. Greeley provides a cultural history of Irish America that is engaging and irreverent. On one level, he surmises that Irish Catholicism, as it has developed in both Ireland and the United States, lost much of its energy by separating itself from its Celtic past and agreeing to be subservient to Rome. Greeley points out that women once enjoyed a greater degree of sexual freedom in the early church and that practices that are not allowed by the church nowadays, such as the ability of clergy to be married, were available in earlier times. Slyly, Greeley reminds us that the cultural legacy is a long one and the further back one goes, the more complex it becomes. Nowadays, we have been trained to think of the church as being a post-Cardinal Cullen phenomenon whereas, in fact, a much different, and a looser, church existed for centuries before the nineteenth century. Greeley, too, pins his faith in the parish and notes that Fr Theodore M. Hesburgh, a former president of the University of Notre Dame, a man that he much admired, was 'still a parish priest who also happen[ed] accidentally to be a university president'.[9] Like Gordon, Greeley places his faith in the lower clergy, in the brilliant but modest priest, in the ordinary Catholic, rather than in the hierarchy. It is among these classes where the church's true legacy is more likely to be found.

Recent events make it necessary to examine Catholicism and its legacy critically and to revisit the work of Greeley and other authors who are able to understand the church, its true history and the various social and historical movements with which it has interacted. One of the most eminent contemporary American Catholic theologians was the Rev Richard McBrien, who recently passed away, and who advocated throughout his career for deep critical examinations of the church. He spoke for 'the ordination of women as priests, the repeal of obligatory celibacy and the acceptance of birth control [and defied] the papal doctrine of infallibility'.[10] At the same time, McBrien, while pushing for change within the church, remained steadfast and orthodox in his faith, 'there is only one Christian faith, but there have been literally thousands of beliefs held and transmitted at one time or another' – some have endured, while others 'have receded beyond the range of vision or even of collective memory'.[11] It must seem that this is the moment for the Irish Catholic Church to reinvent itself in a more egalitarian shape that responds to its own particular history in Ireland.

Many of Maureen Dezell's conclusions are in agreement with what Greeley and McBrien have found. Nevertheless, the American Catholic Church continues to thrive as Timothy O'Meara, retired provost at the University of Notre Dame reminds her, 'there is no place on earth that Catholicism is more alive than on Catholic university campuses', with students enjoying mandatory classes in Theology and involving themselves in 'Catholic social action'.[12] In the US, where major Catholic universities enjoy a large degree of independence from their overseers, a kind of reinvention and détente is in place that allows young people to remain part of, and be welcome in, the church while, at the same time, going their own way on social issues. Given how Irish universities have evolved, such opportunities are less available to Irish Catholics so renewal is more difficult to achieve for many reasons. For American adults beyond universities and out in the world, Dezell provides an example of how the twenty-first century church might look. She focuses on Old St Pat's in Chicago:

> It is laity-centered, geared to young adults – who have a tendency to drift away from organized religion – and linked to Chicago's business, social action, and Irish communities. The church calendar lists regular meetings of a variety of groups – one for 'devotion to Our Lady', one offering divorce support, a

Jewish-Catholic couples group, and a Bible study meeting, along with choir practice, community outreach, and liturgy meetings. Coming up the following month were a Valentine's Day Mass, a civic forum on art as an expression of the sacred, a reading group meeting (*Portrait of the Artist as a Young Man*), and a Celtic St. Patrick's Day Mass followed by an Irish breakfast, a Mass featuring Irish musicians, and Siamsa na Gael: a celebration of the Celtic Arts at Chicago Symphony Center.[13]

Though some of these events might seem like novelties, all are of substance and in keeping with, and made possible by, Catholicism's cultural legacy – a legacy built on faith, inclusiveness, forgiveness, the word as it is read, spoken and sung, discussion and community. At Old St Pat's in Chicago the parish is built on the various interests that parishioners share rather than on narrow clerical dictates.

Last year, in a question and answer session after a reading of hers I attended in Iowa City, Marilynne Robinson said that she thought there was no better explanation available for the reality of our world and humankind than what is found in sacred Christian literature. Her remark reminds us that while we might dispense with the Catholic hierarchy, it would be rash to erase the tradition. Irish religious faith, as I have mentioned, is connected to place, to *dinnseanchas*, in the same manner as Native American faith is. In the Lakota tradition, the original people emerged from Wind Cave in South Dakota and came into the world, thereby establishing this wonderful connection between earth and person. In Ireland, too, land is sacred and has helped shape who we are and what we believe in. To a degree, we Irish take our faith from the land, a land/faith that is encoded in Catholicism. The land, the whole space of Ireland, is sacred in itself and also sanctified by the Catholic Church, and by other faiths and beliefs as Paula Meehan eloquently gives voice to in her interrogation of Marianism:

> Or the grace of a midsummer wedding
> when the earth herself calls out for coupling

> and I would break loose of my stony robes,
> pure blue, pure white, as if they had robbed
> a child's sky for their colour. My being
> cries out to be incarnate, incarnate,
> maculate and tousled in a honeyed bed.[14]

Culture is complex and develops in ways that makes it difficult to dismantle. Whereas, as Auge correctly points out, 'the once imposing edifice of Irish Catholicism appear[s] increasingly derelict', much life is to be found beyond the great stone buildings, and, many of the clergy inside such buildings are men and women of great honour.[15] In language and thought, sign and dream, love and hate, man and woman, boy and girl, the Catholic legacy lingers to enrich and complicate life.

In *Irish Catholicism Since 1950: The Undoing of a Tradition* Louise Fuller defines the role and influence played by the church in Irish life:

> One of the most outstanding features of Irish Catholic culture in the post-independence era was the extent to which the state, by the actions, words and public appearances of its representatives, legitimated the Catholic ethos. An alliance was formed between the Catholic Church authorities and the Free State government during the Civil War years, and W.T. Cosgrave during his tenure of office looked to the Church to augment the authority of the government. The alliance was a mutually reinforcing one. The bishops were prepared to throw their weight behind the new state and endorse its political legitimacy, which was being contested by the anti-Treaty republicans, and the rulers of the new state were not disposed to question the authority of the Church in matters having to do with education, health or sexual morality, traditionally seen by the Church as its area of competence.[16]

The support of the hierarchy lent an additional layer of legitimacy to the new regime and, in return, the church was allowed to influence legislation and action. Though a great deal of the semiotics of this relationship was lost on me as a child growing up in the 1950s and 1960s in County Wexford, one aspect of the relationship between church and state was crystal clear – that the primary power resided in the church. It was a familiar sight in Enniscorthy whenever Bishop Donal Herlihy appeared in public to witness our public figures kowtowing to him. As a child, I remember how easy and approachable our public figures were, how even a boy might accost Mr Sean Browne TD or Mr Andy Doyle, a local councillor and business leader, and demand a word or two. In contrast, Bishop Herlihy was regally unapproachable. Our public figures were of our world, the bishop was from another planet. In the Ferns report, Bishop Herlihy came in for fierce criticism:

> The report's harshest judgments were against Donal Herlihy, the former bishop of Ferns, who has since died, and his successor, Brendan Comiskey, who resigned in 2002 after the BBC broadcast a documentary about Mr. O'Gorman. The Ferns report also touched on the Vatican's demand for secrecy in sexual abuse cases – on pain of excommunication – and revealed how Bishops Herlihy and Comiskey repeatedly placed priests whom they knew to be pedophiles in positions that made it easy for them to abuse children.[17]

Looking back, my sense is that our bishop resided outside of our world. In our rural town, loyalties were to each other and to our own priests, about whom there was no end of discussion and speculation. The regal entrance of the Bishop of Ferns for confirmations and other high liturgical occasions in St Aidan's Cathedral seemed disassociated from our lives of faith; aberration rather than affirmation. The old people I knew and loved referred to the cathedral as 'the chapel' so that it seemed less grand and more of us. It was not difficult for the hierarchy to abandon us because of the degree of separation they had established between their domain and ours. In hindsight, we depended on our bishop's oversight, his remoteness from the day-to-day should have allowed him to understand and quickly root out evil; however, he thought it more important to protect the image of the church than to do what was right.

Richard P. McBrien begins his *Caesar's Coin: Religion and Politics in America* with an excerpt from Lincoln's 'Gettysburg Address' rather than a church homily or quote from the Bible:

> 'Fourscore and seven years ago,' President Abraham Lincoln began, 'our fathers brought forth on this continent a new nation, conceived in liberty, and dedicated to the proposition that all men are created equal.' This book is a book about the American Proposition as it applies to the issue of religion and politics.[18]

An American theologian beginning a history of the relationship between religion and politics with a quotation from a political speech that emphasises liberty and equality makes complete sense in the American context where such tenets as freedom of speech, equality and the separation of church and state are the cornerstones of law and thought. Though God was and remains integral to American thought, no such 'mutually reinforcing' relationship that Fuller finds in Ireland has existed in the United States between church and state, notwithstanding the fact that America's founding fathers were descended from the Pilgrim Fathers. In America, as McBrien points out, religions are connected to public life:

> by what has come to be known as public and/or civil religion, by their common commitment to 'civic republicanism' and to that 'public virtue' which seeks 'to promote the political and social involvement of all citizens'.[19]

In Ireland, both the church and the state, by ceding authority to the church, placed the reputation of the church above the welfare of Ireland's citizens. My sense is that the weakness here lies with the civil authorities who had been elected to provide oversight over the country and its people but who abdicated this responsibility. All organisations, great and small, civil and religious, require oversight. In America, it is, or should be, the 'public good, the real welfare of the great body of the people', James Madison insisted, which is the final measure of any form of government and to which 'the voice of every good citizen' must be reconciled.[20] McBrien reminds us that the blending of ideals and ideologies from church and state can be a positive one so long as some separation is maintained. In Ireland, therefore, we can say that the cultural legacy need not be erased from state matters but that it instead should be at play in a dynamic that McBrien labels as 'civic republicanism'.[21] Writing in 1967, another Irish American priest, Fr James Kavanagh noted that:

> Catholicism as a monolithic structure is disappearing. Once a man who differed with the party line stole quietly away ... He refuses to accept irrelevant sermons, a sterile liturgy, a passé and speculative theology ...[22]

Though the Cloyne and other reports have driven worshipers away from the church, the need for reinvention predates these reports.

Frank McCourt provides an often quoted and provocative declaration at the beginning of *Angela's Ashes*, his best-selling memoir of his family's life in Ireland and America:

> When I look back on my childhood I wonder how I survived at all. It was, of course, a miserable childhood: the happy childhood is hardly worth your while. Worse than the ordinary miserable childhood is the miserable Irish childhood and worse yet is the miserable Irish Catholic childhood.[23]

Published in 1996, at a time when many shocking revelations about the role of the Catholic Church in child abuse were being revealed, McCourt's statement caught something of the *zeitgeist*, albeit in an exaggerated tone. Given all that we have learned in recent decades, it is tempting to discard everything associated with Irish Catholicism, to throw out the baby with the bathwater as it were. Given McCourt's outburst it is no surprise that the Catholic hierarchy in Ireland believed that 'the returned emigrants, on the other hand, also posed a challenge to traditional values and ways of thinking'.[24] The power of the returned emigrant to undermine traditional sexual practices is given eloquent voice in John McGahern's *Amongst Women* in the character of Nell Monahan, a young woman who is home on vacation from America. However, abuse and misery, though they are predominant images and realities of the present, do not negate all of the Catholic light. Part of the journey that McCourt chronicles is the throwing off of Catholicism in favour of freedom and hedonism, an effort that is facilitated by leaving Ireland for America, and described with great comic effect near the close of *Angela's Ashes*:

> She takes my hand and leads me into a bedroom, puts down her glass, locks the door, pushes me down on the bed. She's fumbling at my fly. Damn buttons. Don't you have zippers in Ireland? She pulls out my excitement climbs up on me slides up and down Jesus I'm in heaven and there's a knock on the door the priest Frank are you in there Frieda putting her fingers to her lips and her eyes rolling to heaven Frank are you in there Father would you ever take a good running jump for yourself an oh God oh Thomas do you see what's happening to me at long last and I don't give a fiddler's fart if the Pope himself knocked on this door and the College of Cardinals gathered gawking at the windows.[25]

For McCourt, the various miseries underlining an Irish Catholic upbringing are prerequisites for the independent artistic life.

We should understand though that McCourt does not throw off his upbringing completely; rather, like the relationship that Blake forges between innocence and experience in his work, McCourt's contrasting states – Ireland/America and Catholicism/Hedonism – serve as two sides of a single coin rather than wildly separate opposites. In fact, this excerpt from *Angela's Ashes* pays homage to tradition in its pastiche imitation of the dramatic monologue that Joyce employs in the 'Penelope' episode that concludes *Ulysses*. Ironically, the priest participates in

McCourt's sexual encounter, though from a safe distance, the door dividing him from Frank and Frieda acting as a kind of Atlantic separating America from Ireland. Until recently, the Irish hierarchy's obsession with sexual matters gave the impression that they were always standing guard outside of people's bedrooms like the hapless priest in *Angela's Ashes*, who is not even given a name by McCourt. In the end, it was sex that brought down the church. Irish men and women liked sex so much that they eventually felt confident enough to disregard the church's wishes, while the hierarchy somehow persuaded itself that sexual abuse of children was neither a serious nor a criminal matter.

Though an increasingly maligned and marginalised figure in Ireland, the Irish Catholic priest has received favourable coverage in two recent acclaimed novels by Irish writers: Colm Tóibín's *Brooklyn* (2009) and Colum McCann's *Let the Great World Spin* (2009). Interestingly enough, the two clerical figures in these novels are ministering outside of Ireland – in Brooklyn and the Bronx, respectively. Both resist the image of the stereotypical Irish priest that McCourt favours, while at the same time conforming to another image of the helpful and useful Irish clergyman doing service overseas. Though their missions are outside of Ireland, both Fr Flood in *Brooklyn* and John Corrigan in *Let the Great World Spin* belong to a long-standing process of the Irish Catholic Church intervening overseas for the improvement of the lives of individuals living in far-flung places. Both Flood and Corrigan offer assistance without proselytisation. In addition to making it possible for Eilis Lacey to emigrate to America, his primary role in the plot of *Brooklyn*, Fr Flood encourages Eilis in her pursuit of a third-level education that would been impossible for her to have had access to in Ireland, and in his dealings with her is generally supportive and non-judgmental. He presides over his Brooklyn parish genially and paternally and is more interested in engaging with his parishioners and seeking to help them get what they need, rather than in meddling in their private lives. From America, Fr Flood has learned a degree of tolerance and accommodation that is necessary to prosper and be useful in a quickly changing society. In the 'Baby Boom' years following the Second World War – a time of upward mobility – educational opportunities resulting from the GI Bill increased wealth and helped create a more lively and diverse culture with the result that the American Catholic Church had a fight on its hands to retain the loyalty of its flock. To remain relevant, it could not adopt the heavy-handed tactics of its Irish counterpart that promulgated a Catholic culture infected with what the Rev Liam Ryan, a prominent sociologist, called the 'four deadly sins of Irish Catholicism: an obsession with sexual morality, clerical authoritarianism, anti-intellectualism or at best non-intellectualism, and the creation of a ghetto mentality'.[26]

Ciaran Corrigan notes of his older brother John in *Let the Great World Spin* that:

> he was at the origin of things and I now had a meaning for my brother – he was a crack of light under the door, and yet that door was shut to him.[27]

Corrigan is, as Eóin Flannery has pointed out, a rogue priest who is ministering outside of the traditional church, a man raised on a blend of liberation and traditional theology:

> But the insertion of an Irish character, John Corrigan, as one of the protagonists, arguably the central personality, permits the introduction of religious faith into the narrative. Corrigan's religious vocation, rooted in Catholicism, but gradually receding from its institutional forms, is key to the enactment of redemption in the story ... The lived context of Corrigan's vocation is prostitution and drug addiction; he effectively dwells among a group of black prostitutes in the South Bronx. His dedication to these harassed women is absolute and is tested by repeated physical assaults by pimps, as well as the proximity of the prostitutes' semi-clad, sexualized bodies.[28]

In addition to working with a group of prostitutes, Corrigan also takes groups of senior citizens on day trips. Corrigan falls in love with Adelita in the novel, eventually after much soul-searching agreeing to consummate their relationship. One notices that little divides Corrigan's private and public lives – both of which are defined by patience, kindness and deep generosity. He serves as a link between the priest of the ancient Irish Catholic Church, who was often married and comfortable living among and serving under women, and a priest of the future guided by a mixture of traditional liturgy and the writings of Gustavo Gutiérrez and Ernesto Cardinal, two father-figures of liberation theology who not only resisted oppression by dictators in Central and South America by word and deed but who also pushed back against the Vatican's reprimands of their ways of thinking and leading. One should note, too, that an Irish cleric, albeit a most unconventional one, is at the centre of a great American novel, and a major literary force in healing after 9/11, and after his own martyrdom in a wreck on the East Side Highway. One senses in Corrigan a Christ-like resonance, a power and an influence that endures long after his death. McCann has noted that he:

> wanted for a long time to write about faith and belonging, especially in a radical Catholic context. I wanted a man who would look at the world in all its filth and poverty and yet still believe that, one day, the meek might actually want it.[29]

Corrigan also links Ireland and America with the latter being the diverse place, as in *Angela's Ashes* and *Brooklyn*, where independent and mature experience is possible. Given the climate in Ireland in recent decades and the collapse of the influence and integrity of the church, it would have seemed impossible to Tóibín and McCann, I would guess, to have imagined similar lives for Fr Flood and John Corrigan in Ireland. America, though clerical abuse and cover-ups occurred here with great frequency, offered both authors elements of diversity and reinvention that would have been impossible in Ireland. Both novels shine bright and positive lights on the cultural legacy of Irish Catholicism.

It is my sense of things that the cultural legacy of Irish Catholicism, and its American counterpart, will be tied to, and inseparable from, the abuses of young people committed by clergy and subsequent cover-ups by its hierarchy for a long time to come. In his controversial analysis of the role that ordinary Germans played in the Holocaust, Daniel Jonah Goldhagen notes that 'the Holocaust defines not only the history of Jews during the middle of the twentieth century but also the history of Germans'.[30] Without trying to lessen the impact of the Holocaust by comparing it to a reality that it is quite unlike, one can apply the frame of Goldhagen's thesis to events that occurred in Ireland. Even though, as I have pointed out, many aspects of the cultural legacy of Catholicism are positive and enduring, the abiding reality is one of abuse and horror. Our celebration should be muted. What is most important is that the innocent victims of the church remain in the forefront of our thoughts.

NOTES

1. Andrew J. Auge, *A Chastened Communion: Modern Irish Poetry and Catholicism* (Syracuse University Press, 2013), p. 145.
2. Mary Gordon, 'Getting Here from There: A Writer's Reflections on a Religious Past', *Good Boys and Dead Girls and Other Essays* (Viking, 1991), pp 160–61.
3. *Ibid*, pp 163–64.
4. *Ibid*, p. 175.
5. Fintan O'Toole, *Black Hole, Green Card: The Disappearance of Ireland* (New Island Books, 1994), p. 132.
6. Gordon, *Ibid*, p. 174.
7. Maureen Dezell, *Irish America: Coming into Clover* (Doubleday, 2001), pp 163–75.
8. *Ibid*, p. 175.
9. Fr Andrew M. Greeley, *The Irish Americans: The Rise to Money and Power* (Warner Books, 1981), p. 161.

10. Sam Roberts, 'Rev Richard McBrien, Catholic Firebrand, Dies at 78', *New York Times*, 29 January 2015, p. 17.
11. *Ibid*.
12. Dezell, *Ibid*, p. 165.
13. Dezell, *Ibid*, p. 186.
14. Paula Meehan, 'The Statue of the Virgin at Granard Speaks', *The Man Who Was Marked by Winter* (Gallery Press, 1991, p. 41.
15. Auge, *Ibid*, p. 145.
16. Louise Fuller, *Irish Catholicism Since 1950: The Undoing of a Church* (Gill and Macmillan, 2002), p. 3.
17. Brian Lavery, 'Irish Report on Sexual Abuse Causes Outrage', *New York Times*, 13 November 2005, available: http://www.nytimes.com/2005/11/13/world/europe/irish-report-on-sexual-abuse-by-priests-stokes-outrage.html
18. Richard P. McBrien, *Caesar's Coin: Religion and Politics in America* (Macmillan, 1987), p. vii.
19. *Ibid*, p. ix.
20. *Ibid*.
21. *Ibid*.
22. Fr James Kavanagh, *A Modern Priest Looks at His Outdated Church* (Trident Press, 1967), p. xi.
23. Frank McCourt, *Angela's Ashes* (Scribner, 1996), p. 11.
24. Fuller, *Ibid*, p. 43.
25. Frank McCourt, *Ibid*, p. 361.
26. Fintan O'Toole, *The Lie of the Land: Irish Identities* (Verso, 1997), p. 74.
27. Colum McCann, *Let the Great World Spin* (Random House, 2009), p. 67.
28. Eóin Flannery, *Colum McCann and the Aesthetics of Redemption* (Irish Academic Press, 2011), pp 216–19.
29. Colum McCann, 'A Conversation with Colum McCann and Nathan Englander', *Let the Great World Spin* (Random House, 2009, p. 365.
30. Daniel Jonah Goldhagen, *Hitler's Willing Executioners: Ordinary Germans and the Holocaust* (Knopf, 1996), p. 8.

REFERENCES

Gordon, Mary, *Final Payments* (Anchor, 1978).
McGahern, John, *Amongst Women* (Faber, 1990).
   The Dark (Faber, 1965).
Tóibín, Colm, *Brooklyn* (Scribner, 2009).

Return to Finland:
Robert Creeley, Continental Drift

On my next-to-last day in Finland I set out for Ekenäs, a town of fifteen thousand people, ninety-six kilometers south-west of Helsinki. Six months before, in the Christmas Day edition of the *New York Times*, I had read that 'more than 80 percent of the residents of Ekenäs speak Swedish', and that Swedish speakers constitute about 5% of the population of the country as a whole.[1] Since 1917, when Finland secured its independence from Russia, the rights of the Swedish minority, a much larger minority at that time than today, have been guaranteed in the constitution. Finland, like Ireland, has two national languages and the relationship between the majority and minority languages is as tangled in one country as it is in the other and, despite their respective legal statuses, both minority languages are under pressure and in decline. They should not be, but they are. In Helsinki train station I asked for a ticket to Ekenäs and when I looked at it noticed that it read Tammisaari. Before I could question the clerk, she said, a little too proudly I felt, 'it's Tammisaari in Finnish'.

The previous few days had been spent attending an academic conference, so I felt the need to escape from the city. Also, I thought that walking in the fresh air would allow those things that were racing around my head to settle into thoughts. I had come to Finland to speak on the American poet William Stafford at the University of Helsinki, to seek traces of another American poet, Robert Creeley, who had lived in Helsinki for a short time in the 1980s and who had written both memorably and bitterly about his experiences there, and because I'd enjoyed an earlier visit so much. A few months before undertaking this trip I had become an American citizen, so this journey, my first as an American passport-holder, had some aspect of the landmark or novelty about it. I had not given it much thought beforehand, but the fact of my now being an American citizen affected, in odd and subtle ways, how I thought of myself. Though I lived in the same house and went to the same office each day, I was aware of some new and intangible sense of belonging – a degree of ownership, though one that did not bestow entitlement. At the same time my loyalties were divided – two countries, two continents – though my firmest sense of place continued to tie me to the smaller and more intimate spaces of neighbourhood and town, rather than to more abstract ideas of nations. At another level, and a deeper one, I knew that no such division existed: people and culture connect America to Ireland and Finland. In the literary sphere, Ireland and the United States are interdependent. Our writers feed off theirs and vice-versa. That week in Finland, more than ever, I belonged to both ours and theirs. For me, writing is local and continental rather than national.

Ekenäs was the farthest I had travelled from my Helsinki base and therefore, I thought, a likely location for taking stock of this journey I had undertaken and my new persona as an American. I felt something of what the Finnish writer

Pentti Saarikoski felt when he arrived in Dublin on Bloomsday 1982:

> This is journey's end, I sit in my room at the Ormond in Dublin, gazing out at Anna Livia and the seagulls circling above and the row of houses on the far side. Or not journey's end, it's just that I have been sitting here before, looking out this way.[2]

Saarikoski reminds us that it is foolish to think that we can sit on a bed, stop the clock and, idly almost, take stock. It is a waste of time to imagine that what did not work before can be made to succeed second time round. Though becoming an American citizen had clarified things by squaring the reality of where I had lived for twenty-five years with the travel document I bore, it also, as I was often reminded of on this visit to Helsinki, led to confusion because no one I spoke to believed, or wanted to accept, that I was an American. In fact, I myself was surprised that the immigration officer at the airport did not raise his eyes suspiciously after I had presented him with my passport for inspection on my arrival in Finland.

Two months before I had been seated in a room at the convention centre in Austin, Texas, to hear panellists at the annual Association of Writers and Writing Programs (AWP) conference speak in memory of Robert Creeley who had recently passed away. Over the decades, though hardly systematically, I had read and re-read Creeley's work, the poems and essays in particular. One of my favourites is 'The Rhythm':

> It is all a rhythm,
> from the shutting
> door, to the window
> opening,
>
> the seasons, the sun's
> light, the moon,
> the oceans, the
> growing of things.[3]

This poem exhibits a concise and sharp view of the human condition, one formed in the cold, late-Puritan New England shade and warmed under the sun in Majorca, California and New Mexico. His wit had been refined by Black Mountain and the post-World War II counter-culture. In Creeley's work, the line of Emily Dickinson is engaged with the poetics of Pound, Olson, Williams and others, and with the philosophy of thinkers as varied as Guardieff and Wittgenstein. Beneath a surface that appears simple, almost simplistic perhaps, and casual, there lurks strenuous questionings and hard efforts at engagement with humans and their ideas.

Reading Creeley's poems and essays, one is brought into the heart of the poetry debates that took place in the US in the decades after World War II and which resound today – between a formalist poetic model and a more 'projective' structure, to use the term that Creeley coined. Writing from Bolinas in 1974, Creeley states his position:

> Like many of my contemporaries I felt myself obliged to be an explicit craftsman so as to have defense against the authoritative poetry of my youth – whose persons I'd like now not to recall just that it's taken me so long to forget them. So, from that initial, crotchety purview, I've continued, finding and choosing as heroes men and women who must at this point be familiar to anyone who has read me at all: Williams, Pound, H.D., Stein, Zukofsky, Olson, Duncan, Levertov, Ginsberg, Dorn, Bunting, Wieners, McClure, Whalen, Snyder, Berrigan – and so on, being those I can almost see out the window if I look. Put more simply, there's been a way of doing things which found company with others, and in that company one has found a particular life of insistent and sustaining kind.[4]

I am drawn to Creeley's mixture of independence, resistance and belonging. Working as a poet for over forty years, I continue to be guided by his passionate intelligence. He has provided me with a means of escaping – a ladder raised to my bedroom window – from the rather rigid poetic practices and injunctions that were so prevalent in the Irish literary scene of my youth. At the same time – and this is what his detractors often fail to notice – Creeley's work, as Arthur Ford points out, is technically complex and never quite as projective as it appears. William Stafford's work, as I tried to point out rather hopelessly at the conference, while seemingly casual technically is also rooted in tradition with the depth of thought offset by a more latent gravity of style. An advantage of being a writer and scholar is that when one is engaged with the work of the latter, one is forced to read very patiently, to slow down, to adjust one's consciousness so that the poem or story under consideration begins to glow and give off something of its spirit and mechanism. Today we are tempted to read a poem as we might scan a text message; the demands of scholarship, on the other hand, force us into another continuum of space and time. As was the case in the old days, we learn to write from imitation.

Over the years, I have wondered about Creeley in Placitas, New Mexico, Creeley in Bolinas, California, where Richard Brautigan also lived, and imagined what fun it must all have been with so many writers gathered for weekends of sport. Unfortunately, I never got to meet Creeley or hear him read, except on tape and video. Much of the final phase of Creeley's life was spent in Buffalo, New York representing a return to the cold north, one, from all accounts, he found amenable. I'd had a teacher once who himself had been a student of Creeley in Buffalo, who venerated him, and who railed against Helen Vendler for omitting Creeley from her Oxford anthology of American poetry: he said that there could be no anthology of American poetry without Creeley. Hearing him say this, I had gone back to the poems. Later, I came across Thom Gunn's review of the *Collected Poems* in which he noted that Creeley's 'language has never fit in with the official current notions of the poetic'; even though he finds the language to be 'neutral', at the same time, Gunn finds the poetry to be 'powerful and persuasive'.[5]

Interestingly enough, Gunn enumerates the similarities between the 'rhetorical flatness' of Creeley's poetry and the verse of such early Elizabethans as Barnaby Googe, a further indication of the literary rootedness of post-1945 American poets in the English tradition (syntax and diction, in particular), all of which is so apparent in the work of Olson, Stafford, Duncan and Berryman. It is interesting to note how aspects of Elizabethan English are encoded in contemporary American poetry. Gunn notes Creeley's dogged belief in the narrow, personal world, and finds his best work to be 'fresh and clean'.[6] Exploring his poetics from within, Gunn describes the projective elements in the work – the breaths and emphatic endings; the degree to which so much is qualified and made more complex by Creeley's use of punctuation; and he explores 'the recurrent term of *stumbling* for his poetic procedure':

> My luck
> is your gift,
> my melodious
> breath, my stumbling.[7]

'If one stumbles', Gunn notes, 'led or pushed by impulse, one stumbles into the unforeseen, the accidental. Even so, the accidental may have its patterns'.[8] To come across Creeley for the first time is exciting and challenging. Like Thom Gunn, I was moved by Creeley's work, and remain so, while at the same time, on first reading, I was perplexed by its line, diction and syntax. Initially, I could neither describe his points nor his poetics, not even to myself.

My presence that day in a room in Texas to hear Creeley's friends and admirers speak was no accident, or mere stumbling: a stumbling occurred when I discovered that Creeley had held the Bicentennial Chair in American Studies at the University of Helsinki in 1988–89. At the anniversary banquet celebrating the creation of this position, which I attended as one of the conference participants on my second visit to the city, I looked across the room toward the table where many of the holders of this chair were seated. In the centre of this group of scholars was one creative writer – N. Scott Momaday, the great Kiowa writer – and I felt a rare privilege to be in the same room as the author of *House Made of Dawn* and other works. When the meal had ended, the last speeches had been delivered, and while the group tiredly exited, I lingered a moment as I made my departure, resting my two hands on the back of the chair on which Momaday had sat to give thanks to him, in my own way, for the generosity of spirit displayed in his books. I might have approached him that evening but I thought better of it seeing that he was surrounded by many professors, a majority of this group being political scientists. I would have liked to have seen Robert Creeley seated beside Momaday at the table of the honorees, two writers babbling about the lives and the scrapes they had managed to survive both home and abroad. Though his books remain, Creeley's image had disappeared.

Creeley's 'Autobiography' is appended to Tom Clark's study of the poet's work and is dated Helsinki, Finland, 23 March 1989.[9] At a kind of journey's end in Dublin, Pentti Saarikoski did not manage to gain the hoped for insight because, he felt, that 'one should not return to places associated with cherished memories'.[10] For Creeley, a long way from home, at a kind of journey's end and in a new place, Helsinki provided imaginative opportunities, both in poetry and prose. Helsinki does not figure greatly in the autobiography – there's a brief account of a meeting with Claes Andersson, poet member of Finland's parliament, and, near the end, a description of what is visible from his apartment window – though I have a sense, or perhaps I just imagine it, that the prose takes some elements of its shape from the city.

The early part of the autobiography is written in a complex, highly punctuated prose style, as is the case in many of his poems. This short autobiography, its very compactness in keeping with the modus operandi behind the poetry, teems with personal and literary history and is underlined by apology, description and revision:

> when young I'd written Olson with almost pious exclamation: 'form is never more than an extension of content.' Now I might say equally, 'Content is never more than an extension of form'.[11]

One can only wonder the degree to which the tone, timbre and thoughts present in the autobiography are the result of Creeley's presence in Helsinki. For example, to what extent can we say that the poet's memory of his early life in New England has somehow been filtered through the view from his Helsinki apartment window? When I returned to Helsinki having read the autobiography, I noted the marks Creeley had made on the city and remembered how at the beginning Creeley had teased out his own childhood while at the end, in Helsinki, he had explored that of his children who had been sent out merrily onto the streets to walk to school. Helsinki, I conjectured, was where past, present and future aligned for Robert Creeley.

The Helsinki poems are gathered in *Windows* (1990) and comprise the collection's sixth and final section, entitled 'Helsinki Window'. The starting point is the view from his apartment:

> Old sky freshened with cloud bulk
> slides over frame of window the
> shadings of softened greys a light
> of air up out of this dense high
> structured enclosure of buildings
> top or pushed up flat of bricked roof
> frame I love *I love* the safety of

> small world this door frame back
> of me the panes of simple glass yet
> airy up sweep of birch trees sit in
> flat below all designation declaration
> here as clouds move so simply away.[12]

Like the window—bricks and sky, the parts of the sequence are shaped as rectangular frames that contain aspects of what is visible, and the voice of the speaker, each forming a Black Mountain, projective verse 'field'. The window is the field. Helsinki, for Creeley, is personified by its sky:

> I can watch, from this window, an insistent height of sky that has been all this past fall and winter a companion to my being here, and a subtle, unaggressive information of where, in fact, it is …[13]

that can be both a field itself on which words can be transcribed, and, at its outer edges, the place where one begins and departs:

> there is a broken-record tone of necessity in that it keeps coming back to the beginning of the proposition, that there was someone to begin with, and that something therefore followed.[14]

On the level of metaphor, the window serves Creeley perfectly as it is pliable and can be made to suggest so much: our limited view of the world, the small shape of the poem contrasted with the world's complex contortions, the fact that the viewer is always himself on display and the reality that nothing outside is fixed, that all is subject to change, that one's children walk along the streets to the city tram stop in preparation for the walk into their own independent lives. The room where Creeley writes is the body, 'the someone to begin with', the windows his eyes on the world.

Interviewed by Charles Bernstein, who spoke on the memorial panel to Creeley at the AWP conference in Austin, Creeley noted that:

> the light in Finland was just mind-blowing, whether it was in the diminution of it towards the center of the year, in the winter. But, equally, this vatic light that would then come back at the edge of summer.[15]

In Finland, I too had noticed the light. One morning sailing out from Helsinki toward Tallinn I observed how the light was similar to Irish light and, as a result, how much the rhythms of my mind and body are rooted in the north. I understood that I am of this light, this clear cold space. That morning I experienced the deepest feelings of ecstasy and belonging: to Finland, Ireland and America.

In the summer of 1996, seven years later, Creeley made a return visit to Helsinki to read at the Helsinki Festival. In another essay, sizing up both trips, he noted how much more satisfactory his second had been compared to the first. The occasion of his reading he described as being:

> one of those golden moments for a poet, when he or she can say or do nothing wrongly, when the audience will secure and sustain the music it has come to hear.[16]

Because it was summer, 'people were so instantly handsome, their movement lithe, sensuous, confident. It was lovely. No place I came to seemed apart from its spell'.[17] His Fulbright visit had ended before summer had begun and throughout served to reinforce Creeley's 'impatience and displacement' and made him feel 'more isolated than ever'.[18] At the root of his unhappiness was the winter. The temperatures seemed to hover around freezing (unseasonably mild for Finland) so that the ice rinks never froze enough for his kids to skate in anything better than slush, and he decried the shortness of winter days in the far north. Certainly, *kaamos*, the dark-blue glow of the polar night, was not for him:

> the days, of course, had grown ironically to only a few hours of light, and now the night's blackness prevailed for hours and hours on end. We rose in the dark, and by mid-afternoon it was dark again. Why did we get up at all?[19]

Everything in the north is transformed by summer – from the moods and faces of the inhabitants, to the landscapes that define us all. Creeley's complaints in winter and rejoicings in summer seem Irish to me; even the freakish winter weather he experienced in Finland is a dead ringer for the damp Irish winter through which one is often cold and dispirited. Creeley's unhappiness on his Fulbright year is further explained by his poor physical state on arrival:

> I arrived with both feet crippled from a recent operation to free the joints of my big toes on either foot, locked as they'd been with arthritis. So, together with patient family attending, I was wheeled out of the airport, into a car, then taken to what was to be our home in Helsinki, a generously provided apartment just up from the Forum and the railroad station.[20]

Clearly, given his condition, he had chosen the wrong year to winter in Finland. His attitude to the weather is underlined by, or even explained by, his claim to 'being part Irish myself'.[21] Of course, this harsh tone is diluted later on when he speaks in hindsight to Bernstein. It was only later from reading Daniel Tobin's scholarship that I began to understand how Irish Creeley actually was, how connected we were:

> Then, when at last I was twenty-one,
> my mother finally told me
> indeed the name *Creeley* was Irish –
>
> and heavens opened, birds sang,
> and the trees and ladies spoke
> with wondrous voices. The power of the glory
> of poetry – was at last mine.[22]

I had loved Creeley's work long before learning of his connection to Ireland and this new knowledge did not make me feel that I should admire him even more. I suppose, out of a loyalty to American poetry, I bristled at the romantic notion that Creeley pushed connecting Ireland to the essence of verse. On the other hand, I liked how things came together, how language formed countries and tied continents together.

The hours of working on poems in his apartment and the window through which Creeley looked outside and which gave the volume of poems its title are both described, 'I wrote at odd times of the day and night in the small study just off the kitchen. It's one window faced out to the apartment block's inner courtyard'.[23] He notes that his teaching assignment at the university was a 'farce', finds that Finns (the great poet Paavo Haavikko included) do not consider American writing to be of much interest, and he makes so many trips outside of the country, including several returns to the United States, that one wonders if he had been living in Finland at all. The poets he finds common ground with in Finland write in Swedish. Except for the celebration of summer in Helsinki, and the notes he provides on his own working routine as a poet, the essay is embittered in tone. Even so, given my own sad experience of trying to explain Stafford's vision at the conference (in the same building where Creeley had taught), I am heartened by his account of how difficult he found it to get Levertov's and Olson's ideas and poetics across to his students at the University of Helsinki; at the same time, I read 'Coming Home' with misgivings. About Finnish readers' attitude to American writing, Creeley is wrong. In my experience, Finns do appreciate American writing, are in awe of American literary achievement, and the Renvall Institute at the University of Helsinki is a warm space for the American writer. Wandering around Helsinki's streets, stepping in and out of cathedrals, churches, cafes and bars, I felt none of the loathing that Creeley expresses. On the contrary, I was blissfully happy way up north in the light. I was home.

In *Self Portrait*, the Irish poet Patrick Kavanagh writes about going away and returning home, seeing them as two modes of simplicity:

> there are two kinds of simplicity, the simplicity of going away and the simplicity of return. The last is the ultimate in sophistication. In the final simplicity we don't care whether we appear foolish or not. We talk of things that earlier would embarrass. We are satisfied with being ourselves, however small.[24]

Kavanagh is describing the transformation that took place in his outlook to life and poetry while he was recovering from lung cancer, a shift that produced a remarkable synthesis in his work. More generally, he implies that the journey garners for the traveller a newfound confidence that allows him/her to be veiled behind the mask of experience on returning home. For Creeley, who quotes this passage in his essay on Kavanagh, the going away from America (after surgery) was not simple: it was literally a stumbling.

His return to America from his Fulbright, given the hostility he often felt in Finland and his sense that neither he nor his literature was taken seriously by the Finns, was simple: it was a return to what was known, to a place where he had prestige. I wonder why he felt the Finns were so reluctant to praise American writing – was it because Creeley sought their affirmation too eagerly? Or because America seemed to lead at everything else – business, technology, medicine, space exploration, film – could it be that the Finns were reluctant to assent to the fact that America was also the leader of literature? If so, what was left for the rest of the world? For Creeley, the final simplicity was his return trip: he enjoyed good weather and was feted as a poet. Kavanagh has written that 'real technique is a spiritual quality, a condition of mind, or an ability to invoke a particular condition of mind' – qualities both Creeley and Kavanagh possessed in abundance.[25] Retreating to the US from Helsinki for a second time, I recall Italo Calvino's maxim, 'the city exists and it has a simple secret: it knows only departures, not returns'.[26] It defines my return more than it does Creeley's, his being closer to what Kavanagh describes. Landing in JFK, I stood in the shorter of the two lines in front of a sign that read: US CITIZENS. Handing over my passport at the desk, I was aware of my own multiple sense of belonging: I am home on two continents, stumbling into languages: oral, written, connected.

NOTES

1. Lizette Alvarez, 'Finland Makes its Swedes Feel at Home', *New York Times*, 25 December 2005, http://www.nytimes.com/2005/12/25/world/europe/finland-makes-its-swedes-feel-at-home.html.
2. Pentti Saarikoski, *The Edge of Europe: A Kinetic Image*, translated by Anselm Hollo (Action Books, 2007), p. 160.
3. Robert Creeley, *Selected Poems* (University of California Press, 1991), p. 90.
4. Robert Creeley, *Was That a Real Poem and Other Essays*, edited by Donald Allen (Four Seasons Foundation, 1979), p. 100.
5. Thom Gunn, *Shelf Life: Essays, Memoirs and an Interview* (Faber, 1994), p. 87.
6. *Ibid*, p. 91.
7. *Ibid*, p. 88.
8. *Ibid*, pp 88–9.
9. Tom Clark, *Robert Creeley and the Genius of the American Commonplace* (New Directions, 1993), pp 122–44.
10. Saarikoski, *Ibid*, p. 161.
11. Clark, *Ibid*, p. 142.
12. Robert Creeley, *Windows* (New Directions, 1990), p. 136.
13. Creeley, pp 37–8.
14. Clark, *Ibid*, pp 143–44.
15. Robert Creeley, 'Interview with Charles Bernstein', *Just in Time: Poems 1984–1994* (New Directions, 2001), p. 31.
16. Robert Creeley, 'Coming Home', *Books from Finland*, Vol. 1, 1997, p. 38.
17. *Ibid*, 37–8.
18. *Ibid*, p. 35.
19. *Ibid*, p. 31.
20. *Ibid*.
21. *Ibid*.
22. Robert Creeley, 'Theresa's Friends', *So There: Poems 1976–83* (New Directions, 2001), p. 139.
23. 'Coming Home', *Ibid*, p. 36.

24 Patrick Kavanagh, *A Poet's Country: Selected Prose,* edited by Antoinette Quinn (Lilliput Press, 2003), p. 314.
25 *Ibid*, p. 278.
26 Italo Calvino, *Invisible Cities,* translated by William Weaver (Harcourt, 1974), p. 56.

REFERENCES

Creeley, Robert, *Just in Time: Poems 1984–1994* (New Directions, 2001).
'A True Poet' in Peter Kavanagh (ed.), *Patrick Kavanagh: Man and Poet* (National Poetry Foundation/University of Maine at Orono, 1986, pp 311–14).
Ford, Arthur, *Robert Creeley* (Twayne, 1978).
Tobin, Daniel, *Irish American Poetry from the Eighteenth Century to the Present* (University of Notre Dame Press, 2007).

THE HABIT OF LAND:
EAVAN BOLAND'S IRISH AMERICAN VOICE

One of the most heart-wrenching moments in Eavan Boland's work is located in the 'A Fragment of Exile' chapter in *Object Lessons: The Life of a Woman and the Poet in Our Time*, her 1995 volume of memoir, family history and a recounting of life in the poetry business and among poets. At the outset, in a voice that reaches from the present back into childhood, Boland describes, in the plain, understated speech of the obituary, her moment of separation from Ireland and, perhaps, from childhood:

> I had no choice. That may well be the first, the most enduring characteristic of influence. What's more, I knew nothing. One morning I was woken before dawn, dressed in a pink cardigan and skirt, put in a car, taken to an airport. I was five. My mother was with me. The light of the control tower at Collinstown Airport – it would become Dublin Airport – came through the autumn darkness. I was sick on the plane, suddenly and neatly, into the paper bag provided for the purpose.[1]

Though fortunate to have enjoyed a privileged upbringing – as her biography makes clear – as the daughter of a diplomat and an artist raised in a secure, loving and well-connected family, Boland, like all children, was not the director of her own life; instead, entrusted into her parents' care, she was brought to London and then New York, the family group following the father's overseas postings.[2] For many migrants, shunted from one location to another, the new country will often offer little improvement on the place that had been left behind; Boland, however, was transported from one safe environment to another. Nevertheless, as she has documented in her poetry and prose, her removal from Ireland was traumatic and has had a profound effect on how she understands the world. 'Exile', she points out, 'is not simple', and can be felt equally, though nuanced differently, across race, gender, nationality and social class.[3] In addition, one would suppose, there will always be something impermanent for the child about the ambassador's residence, the sense that, for all of its seeming luxury and prestige, it is a temporary dwelling rather than a home; that its rooms, just when they become familiar, will be handed over to others. Post-war London, a city of derelict buildings where wartime food rationing continued until 1954, was hardly glamorous. British children of this period, as Dominic Sandbrook reminds us:

> still wondered what their parents meant when they reminisced about eating oranges, pineapples and chocolate; they bathed in a few inches of water, and wore cheap, threadbare clothes with 'Utility' labels.[4]

The Boland family's living conditions and arrangements were rather cold, particularly when contrasted with the warm atmosphere of the Dublin home they had left behind:

> After the domestic warmth of the family home in Lesson Park, the embassy seemed austere by comparison, a 'compartmentalized' state reception building as opposed to a home ... Upstairs, one side of the building looked out over the grounds of Buckingham Palace, where the young Irish girl, who sometimes watched Prince Charles play with his nanny, turned an armchair over on its side and rode it 'away from

this strange house' with its 'fiction of home in the carpets on the floor'. At home, the upstairs rooms where the family lived seemed cold after the intimacy of the children's lives in the family home in Dublin.[5]

The flight from Ireland, therefore, is an exit from the security of childhood, as well as a breaking of the connection with place. Though young, Boland must begin to find her way in the world as an adult might, and seek to deflect, as has often been the experience of the Irish overseas, points of view voiced to make her feel, simultaneously, inferior and Irish:

> [...] becoming the language of the country that
> I came to in nineteen-fifty-one:
> barely-gelled, a freckled six-year-old,
> overdressed and sick on the plane
> when all of England to an Irish child
>
> was nothing more than what you'd lost and how:
> was the teacher in the London convent who
> when I produced 'I amn't' in the classroom
> turned and said – 'you're not in Ireland now'.[6]

The Irish voice is borne by distinct accents and it is telling that Boland, who as an adult would become a poet of resistance and empowerment, recalls an insult that goes to the heart of language, nationality and identity. For Boland, as a writer, exile will be a significant influence on her life and work. Irish people inherit 'emigrant songs which make it [exile] sound so simple; they speak of green shores and farewells' though what is handed down does not quite fit the nuances and cadences brought on by separation.[7] A priority in Boland's work is to provide an account of exile that is realistic, personal and rooted in contemporary times.

The trauma revealed in Boland's account of her involuntary departure from Ireland can be gauged by how deeply ingrained its details have been soldered into her poetry and prose. The vomiting on the airplane is a reminder that exile is equally physical and psychic, with the body responding in its own manner to being removed from its native and natural place. In Boland's poetry, particularly in such extended meditations as 'Anna Liffey', we are always aware of the passion and power that is invested in Dublin as the city being recovered as we – poet and readers – search for the markers of lost time:

> I came here in a cold winter.
>
> I had no children. No country.
> I did not know the name for my own life.
>
> My country took hold of me.
> My children were born.
>
> I walked out in a summer dusk
> To call them in.
>
> One name. Then the other one.
> The beautiful vowels sounding out home.[8]

Boland, living in Dublin as a grown woman, writes with the passionate commitment of a returned exile though she does so without unwarranted sentiment. Her fierce embrace of suburbia, for example, marks one of her original contributions to Irish writing. In *Brooklyn*, Colm Tóibín, through his protagonist Eilis Lacey, explores a similar sense of the physical revulsion brought on by the rawness of displacement:

> ... she had no idea how far under the sea she was except that her cabin was deep in the belly of the ship. As her stomach began dry heaves, she realized that she would never be able to tell anyone how sick she felt. She pictured her mother standing at the door as the car took her and Rose to the railway station ...[9]

Though Tóibín's portrait is more visceral than Boland's, this is the result of Eilis's journey to America being undertaken by boat on a rough sea in contrast to the brief plane ride that Boland describes. In *Brooklyn*, as in many representations of exile in Irish and Irish American writing, *choice* is complex. Boland had no choice but to travel with her family to London; in her journey we can observe both the luxury of being drawn away from a narrow parochial world into a wider cosmopolitan one as well as the pain that Boland recounts in *Object Lessons* and in her poetry. Eilis Lacey's situation is equally complex. Although she does choose to leave County Wexford for New York, she is quite a passive young woman with the result that her emigration is engineered by Fr Flood rather than pressed by her own desires. Fr Flood is an energetic Irish priest who oversees a parish in New York and is a mover and shaker who has established many connections throughout his parish's hinterland – his power is difficult to resist. Eilis understands that she is not likely to enjoy good job opportunities at home and she is also the second and least-favoured sister, both sharing a house with their widowed mother. Eilis, like many American immigrants, would probably have preferred to remain at home, though she makes the decision to leave in the face of economic necessity – among other reasons. In the period before her departure, Eilis resolves to pretend:

> ... at all times that she was filled with excitement at the great adventure on which she was ready to embark. She would make them believe, if she could, that she was looking forward to America and leaving home for the first time. She promised herself that not for one moment would she give them the smallest hint of how she felt, and she would keep it from herself if she had to until she was away from home.[10]

Whether such life-altering decisions are being made on one's own behalf or on behalf of a child, necessity and choice can never be made congruent. Though *Object Lessons* and *Brooklyn* are explorations of the lives of quite different women composed in distinct literary genres, they both hinge on defining moments of separation from Ireland, moments that linger long into the future. How such events manifest themselves as lifelong gyres is defined clearly by Alistair MacLeod in one of his short stories:

> Something like when you cut your hand with a knife by accident, and even as you're trying to staunch the blood flowing out of the wound, you know the wound will never really heal totally and your hand will never look quite the same again. You can imagine the scar tissue that will form and be a different color and texture from the rest of your skin.[11]

In Boland's poetry and prose and in Tóibín's and MacLeod's fiction, great interest is expressed in the theme of exile from islands and areas close to the sea – Ireland and Nova Scotia – though there is equal importance given to the complex issue of return. Perhaps the exile has had no choice but to leave, but the manner of departure does not preclude the positive influence that life in the new place will have on the formation of the exiled woman or man. The exile/emigrant/immigrant scar is complex; on the one hand, it can be a marker of enduring pain while on the other it can equally signify independence, growth and liberation. It is often the case that an individual will experience both in oscillating waves.

Jody Allen Randolph has provided a chronology of Boland's childhood spent overseas (though she and Boland differ on the age of Eavan upon leaving Dublin for London):

> Boland, who was born in 1944 in Dublin, lived in London from the ages of five or six to eleven; she then lived in New York City from ages eleven to fourteen when she returned to Dublin to attend school, 'her mother enrolled her in the Holy Child Convent in Killiney ... in order to pass the GCSE'.[12]

The tone Boland uses to describe this return to Dublin, compared to that utilised in the narrative of her departure nearly a decade before, is open and expansive and a narrative of deliverance:

> I came back to Ireland when I was fourteen. I saw unfamiliar sights: horses and lamplight and the muddy curve of the Liffey. I grew to know street names and bus timetables. I went to live with my sisters in a flat outside the city. I went to boarding school. I studied for exams. I started to explore the

word Irish, not this time as a distant fact but as a close-up reality of my surroundings. As a word which painted letter boxes and colored trains. Which framed laws and structured language.[13]

Later, in 'A Habitable Grief', a poem from *The Lost Land* (1998), she casts light on what she has brought back with her from exile:

Long ago
I was child in a strange country:

I was Irish in England.

I learned
a second language there
which has stood me in good stead –

the lingua franca of a lost land.[14]

Two of the impulses that drive Boland's artistic enterprise are the desire to recreate what has been lost, personally and nationally, by exclusion and exile, and the need to communicate what she has absorbed from displacement for the benefit of others. In *Brooklyn* Tóibín represents this same process though in another way: what Eilis has absorbed from New York is identified by others in her hometown when she returns there upon her sister's death. It is arguable that Eilis's transformation is more superficial than the one that Boland describes in *A Lost Land* and elsewhere; hers is an influence communicated by look and gesture rather than through language, the given medium of the writer.

Writing in his introduction to *Ireland in Exile: Irish Writers Abroad*, his 1993 anthology of Irish writers living overseas, Dermot Bolger noted that nowadays 'Irish writers no longer go into exile, they simply commute' and that 'while editing this anthology my major problem was remembering who was now back and who was away'.[15]

On one level, Bolger's hypothesis makes sense because it is certainly a fact that Irish writers, like many Irish living overseas who follow a variety of professions, wander back-and-forth between Ireland and sundry international destinations. From construction workers to diplomats to writers, we can trace patterns of years or decades spent in the US or elsewhere that are broken up, or linked, by years spent in Ireland. Many Irish writers have either emigrated to America, or have spent considerable periods of time there. These writers can be divided into two main groupings: established writers who have come to the US to take up top-tier university appointments such as Seamus Heaney, Paul Muldoon, Thomas Kinsella and Colm Tóibín, to name a few, and writers who have come to America as more fledgling artists: Colum McCann, Greg Delanty, Mary O'Donoghue, Belinda McKeon and others. In this regard, Boland is more difficult to place. Her appointment at Stanford University, where she serves as Bella Mabury and Eloise Mabury Knapp, Professor in Humanities and Director of Creative Writing, is a prestigious one; however, she is also a writer who, because she spent such important formative years in New York, has been shaped as a child by immersion in American place.

At fourteen, Boland moved with her family again, this time to Manhattan. In *Object Lessons* she describes looking out the window from her new home:

> sixteen stories down, the East River flows towards the city. The freighters and barges make their way across a surface where light is broken up into patches and squares of dazzle.[16]

Unlike the London of her childhood, New York was a place Boland grew to appreciate, 'with its finned cars and theatrical weather. The carousel in Central Park. The metal-colored freeze-up of the lake. The bricks too hot to walk on in summer'.[17] Picking up the habits of American teenagers, Boland describes eating hot dogs and listening to Buddy Holly songs and, in a poem by the same title, 'watching old movies when they were new'. Her poems

'Lights', 'The Carousel in the Park' and 'Traveler' all relate to events from this period of her life.[18]

It is unlikely that any Irish writer, no matter if she/he is raised in Ireland or elsewhere, will remain untouched by American cultural and literary influence – the American reach is so pervasive. In Boland's case, to have spent part of her adolescence in New York was to have had a privileged opportunity to absorb and to understand America first-hand. In this respect, Boland's experience is more akin to that of John Montague's and Padraic Fiacc's than to such writers as Muldoon and McKeon given the importance of childhood and adolescence in the individual's formation. Montague was born in Brooklyn in 1929 and returned to Ireland to be raised by relatives in 1933 while Fiacc was born in Belfast in 1924 and raised in Hell's Kitchen in New York from 1929 until 1946 when he returned to Belfast. For all three poets, an American childhood was a part of their upbringing and independence a feature of their work as is clear from Montague's *The Rough Field* (1972),[19] Fiacc's *The Wearing of the Black* (1974),[20] and Boland's poetry and prose. Guinn Batten has written of *The Rough Field* that it:

> is an exile's, and an orphan's, elegiac farewell, a passage from private attachment to the public performance that may at last seal the tomb of the dead and the past. Such a working through of attachment, as Freud has observed, is necessary if the melancholic son – or, one might argue, nation – is to work through the inevitable traumas that characterize the childhood of the orphan as they do the infancy of so many modern states.[21]

Gerald Dawe has written of Fiacc's 'troubled and broken course' as an important governing factor in his work and psychology and these are also aspects of his back-and-forth early life between Ireland and America that stand as foundation stones of his aesthetic and moral viewpoints.[22] In his poems of The Troubles Fiacc's gaze shakes like a lantern in the breeze from Belfast to New York and back again, particularly when his own family's experiences are captured in poems:

> Our father who art a Belfast night
> -pub bouncer had to have
> A bodyguard, drilled recruits for
> The IRA behind the scullery door in
> The black back yard,
>   died
> In your sleep, in silence like
> The peasant you stayed
> Never belonging on Wall Street,
> Your patience a vice
> Catching as a drug![23]

Like Boland's, Fiacc's mature work adopts a freer, more American, literary idiom and structures. A liberated form allows for liberated thought, both mediated by American experience. Montague's specific trauma was caused by being removed from his parents' care in Brooklyn to be raised by relatives in County Tyrone. Like the McCourt family in *Angela's Ashes*, the Montague family was caught up in and undermined by the cruel mechanics of the Great Depression.[24] As Batten points out, Montague's response to place, history, home and return has been influenced by his own childhood removal. Both Montague and Boland share histories of dislocation, though they are quite different in nature in important respects that underpin their work. These writers bring to Ireland wider and alternatively-tuned registers of thought, feeling and morality as legacies of the types of experiences that were just unavailable to people of their particular generations living in Ireland – in Boland's case, being a young woman in New York at the beginning of the women's movement, at its very epicentre, was hugely influential because it gave her something new and important to bring back to Ireland.

One reason why Boland is such an interesting writer is that she is difficult to categorise. In fact, a problem with her reception, influence and importance as a writer of poetry and prose has resulted from the fact that many scholars and critics have chosen to define her too narrowly, particularly in Ireland. Boland's years spent as an adolescent in New York combined with her many subsequent and continuing visits to America align her with the Irish diaspora in general and Irish America in particular, with ample evidence of both present in her work. To put this in context, we can contrast Boland and F. Scott Fitzgerald. The latter, who was born into an Irish American family in St Paul, Minnesota, wrote many great novels and short stories with barely a reference to Irish American experience whereas Boland, an Irish writer, has made this same experience that Fitzgerald ignores a recurring concern in her work. It is not the writer's place of birth that is important; instead, we must look at the kinds of experiences that authors embrace rather than the places where they were born. Wallace Stevens was neither of Irish background nor did he visit Ireland though he engaged with it through his correspondence with Thomas McGreevy and wrote such memorable poems as 'Our Stars Come from Ireland' and 'The Irish Cliffs of Moher', both intense engagements with Irish time and space.[25] We are not accustomed to thinking of Marianne Moore as being Irish or Irish American until perhaps we come to the final stanza of 'Spenser's Ireland' and note:

... The Irish say your trouble is their
trouble and your
               joy their joy? I wish
I could believe it;
     I am troubled, I'm dissatisfied, I'm Irish[26]

Boland returned to Ireland in 1958 and remained there until 1996 when she took up her appointment as a professor of English at Stanford University. She currently divides her time between California and Dublin.[27] Of course, she made frequent and at times extended visits to the US between 1958 and 1996 that are reflected in some of her best poems, notably 'Love' and 'In a Bad Light', both published in *In a Time of Violence* (1994). Among the American universities where Boland served as a visiting professor, or held fellowships, are Bowdoin College, the University of Iowa, the University of Utah and Washington University in St Louis, as well as travelling to many other university campuses and cities to give readings. Today, outside of term-time at Stanford, Boland resides in Dublin. It should be noted that the chronology of composition and publication of Boland's American poems does not always match the experience described in the poem with 'Love' being a good example of this. The poem, first published in *The New Yorker*, appears in the middle section of *In a Time of Violence* (1994), though the events that gave rise to the poem occurred in Iowa City in 1979 where Boland and her husband Kevin Casey had travelled to serve as fellows of the University of Iowa's International Writing Program. While in Iowa, their second child was for a time 'gravely ill with meningitis'.[28] 'Love' is one of Boland's most memorable poems in which so many strands of life and literature are brought together. It is a poem that is set at the centre of things (Iowa) in the middle of America, in a city where the writer's life is honoured (Iowa City, a UNESCO City of Literature), and where a family of four away from Ireland had found deep ground:

> Dark falls on this mid-western town
> where we once lived when myths collided.
> Dusk has hidden the bridge in the river
> which slides and deepens
> to become the water
> the hero crossed on his way to hell.[29]

The illness and recovery of a child is a signal event in the life of a parent and this explains why the experience remained alive and why the poem was written many years later. Also, writers frequently take a long pause before transposing raw material into literary work. In Boland's case, it seems that America has always been a dynamic presence in her life (and hence her work) since she first experienced it first-hand as a teenager and that it has flown into and through her other lives, places and contexts. In addition to being a love poem to family, 'Love' is also a love poem to place – in this instance, Iowa City. Jody Allen Randolph categorises Boland's connection to America as being organic and positive:

> For the first time Boland heard stories of Irish families who had left their country and come to the United States. Her mother took her to see the port where Irish immigrants arrived from Liverpool and Cobh. For the first time, also, Boland could open her mind to the idea that such migrations might not mean displacement but a new sense of place ... Later, as Boland's preface to *A Journey with Two Maps* reveals, she was able to use her American experience as a secondary location, a widening of identity that allowed her to think of American poetry as well as Irish poetry: 'Long before I came to divide my time between California and Dublin I located myself on common ground: in American poetry as well as Irish'.[30]

To remain energetic, Irish literary culture has always required strong measures of influence imported from abroad. One great service that Boland has provided to Irish poetry is that she brought so much back to Ireland from the US. At times, such retrievals can be essentialised and gendered. It might be argued that Boland's interest in, and championing of, such poets as Adrienne Rich, Denise Levertov and Sylvia Plath serves a narrow agenda – that of promoting the work of women poets. To take this route is incorrect: Eavan Boland's practice and example benefits all Irish poets. All poets can learn from reading these three fine poets, as all poets can learn from reading James Wright, Charles Wright and W.S. Merwin. Certainly, the American poets that Boland has sought to promote are often women; however, they are always full of quality and interest. Many of these American poets, like Boland herself in her mature work, challenge the formalist conceits that have underlined Irish and American poetry and it is vital that such voices be heard and that orthodoxy be challenged. Recently, both Eavan Boland and Colm Tóibín have described themselves as writers who divide their time between the US and Ireland, or more precisely, and perhaps more tellingly, between Stanford and Ireland and New York and Ireland, respectively. Such constructions in no way indicate diminished levels of engagement with Ireland; today, as a result of how frequent and complex migration and travel have become, individuals develop deep and complex allegiances to places rather than to one singular place. As readers and critics in the field of Irish Studies, it is important that we allow clear spaces for such ranges of endeavours and attachments so that the work of writers like Boland, Tóibín and others is allowed to prosper and be understood for what it is. Given her various encounters with the United States from adolescence to the present and the nature of her American experience Boland is a unique figure in Irish American poetry.

From 'Migration' through 'Exile, Exile', the first poem from *New Territory* (1967) and the second from *Against Love Poetry* (2001) Boland has explored the experience of the Irish diaspora both directly and indirectly in America. Even in *Domestic Violence* (2007), 'Traveler' and 'How the Dance Came to the City' address aspects of the emigrant experience: the former is a New York poem and the latter a reading of Dublin as a city of departure and return. Some poems directly address Irish American experience while others, such as 'Migration', we can attribute to this subject matter. For the most part, Boland's work on diasporic themes is found in *In Her Own Image* (1980) and the books that follow it. Though 'Migration' is an exception, Boland's Irish American poems are written in the more open forms that she absorbed from contemporary American poetry while at the same time, when needed, retaining the formal patterns of her early work. A vital influence linking both aspects of Boland's career – work published before and after 1980, is that of Sylvia Plath. Both poets get to the point quickly in their work and honour precision and conciseness over elaboration and wordiness. As they achieve a simplicity of diction, image, line and voice, elegance and truthfulness builds. Trans-Atlantic migration is also an important and enabling aspect of Plath's own literary career. Among Boland's notable Irish American poems are 'After a Childhood Away from Ireland' (*Night Feed*, 1982); 'The Emigrant Irish' (*The Journey and Other Poems*, 1986); 'The River', 'In Exile', 'Ghost Stories' (*Outside History*, 1990); 'That the Science of Cartography is Limited', 'In a Bad Light', 'Love' (*In a Time of Violence*, 1994); 'Home' (*The Lost Land*, 1998); 'Exile! Exile!', 'Emigrant Letters' (*Against Love Poetry*, 2001), and 'Traveler' (*Domestic Violence*, 2007). Although relatively few in number, these poems are high in quality and range across Boland's long and productive career. Boland's Irish American poems are among her most anthologised. Daniel Tobin includes four poems in *The Book of Irish American Poetry: From the Eighteenth Century to the Present*, his comprehensive anthology of Irish American poetry where Boland's work sits alongside Montague's, Mahon's, Fiacc's, Muldoon's, O'Donoghue's, Delanty's and other poets generally considered to be Irish rather than Irish American. Despite such evidence from both her work and its reception, Boland is not often cited as an Irish American poet. She has been categorised as a poet of suburbia, of Dublin, as an Irish and British poet, an Anglophone postcolonial poet, a woman poet associated with Adrienne Rich and Denise Levertov, a poet of place, a poet of revision, among other designations, but rarely as an Irish American poet. My own sense of Boland's work is that her great run of success as a poet begins with *In a Time of Violence* (1994) and extends to *Domestic Violence* (2007). As I have pointed out, the volumes that appeared during this time span include work dealing with the Irish American experience as both personal and diasporic history and can be counted among the best poems that Boland has written.

Boland's work belongs in and is central to the Irish-American canon. A significant reason her poetry has not been spoken of more in this context, outside of Irish American academic circles, has been because the field itself, or designation, has just recently begun to emerge more fully into the light as a result of work undertaken by Charles Fanning and Daniel Tobin. In the first edition of his landmark scholarly work, *The Irish Voice in America* (1990), Charles Fanning explains why he has omitted a discussion of poetry from his study:

> And yet, there have been few memorable Irish American poems, especially before very recent times. The problem has been an endemic blight of programmatic melancholy or bravado that emerged from the experience and perception of forced exile. The stock-in-trade of Irish American poetry has been the immigrant's lament for a lost, idealized homeland and the patriot's plea for Irish freedom from British oppression. Such materials make good songs but bad verse that exhibits simplistic strains of nostalgia or righteous indignation.[31]

Fanning's bleak summary neither entices the reader to read such work nor attracts poets who seek to be grouped under such a designation. In Fanning's view, Irish American poetry looked like a thematic and formal ruin. However, a decade later, in the revised and updated version of *The Irish Voice in America*, he reverses course and notes 'the coming of age of Irish American poetry' as the result of the appearance of a younger generation of poets emerging both from Irish America and from first-generation immigrants from Ireland.[32] While both Fanning and Tobin acknowledge that there are great bolts of weak Irish American poetry, it can also be said that much of Irish American poetry is of great value, if our sense of what Irish American poetry is can be expanded. Daniel Tobin points out that:

> Irish American poetry has not yet been sufficiently acknowledged or explored either for its continuities with the poetry of the homeland or for its own continuities and discontinuities or for its potent affinities with other diaspora literatures.[33]

What happens when we take Tobin's direction is quite startling; in addition to the abundance of bad verse that Fanning located, we also become aware of the work of important poets whose connections to Ireland are more oblique though in no way diminished by this fact: Robinson Jeffers, Marianne Moore, Wallace Stevens, Lola Ridge and Robert Creeley, to provide but a few examples of poets whose work appears alongside Eavan Boland's in the *Book of Irish American Poetry*. It is easy to acknowledge that one's connection to place today is complicated by either forced or chosen mobility, but we learn from Tobin's research into the lives, backgrounds and work of American poets how this is hardly something new. By definition perhaps, given the necessity to assimilate into American cultural identity that is a condition of living in the United States, important connections to Ireland have been forced beneath the surface. It is just as easy – perhaps easier – for American writers than for their Irish equivalents to own various and complex allegiances to place, including Ireland. A feature of Tobin's work has been his recovery of hidden Irish American voices, such as Lola Ridge. Like Boland in 'That the Science of Cartography is Limited', Tobin seeks to show that how a discipline is mapped – openly or narrowly – determines our understanding of it:

> -and not simply by the fact that this shading of
> forest cannot show the fragrance of balsam,
> the gloom of cypresses
> is what I wish to prove.[34]

Cartography, emerging from China, had initially served as a function of military/colonial powers and as an aid to conquest. From maps much has been excluded. Literary anthologies, maps of another kind, have also operated in a similar manner, to which both Boland and Tobin stand in opposition. In Boland's case, the continuities and discontinuities that Tobin sees as being fundamental to our understanding of an expanded Irish American poetry are equally appropriate places to begin a discussion of her work in general.

Throughout Boland's Irish American poetry, one finds ebbs and flows and motions back and forth between human engagement with America and with the emigrant life as a personal and national experience, though both are often linked in her work. Of course, her Irish and American lives cannot be separated as they both inform her work, despite the theme or location of the poem. Furthermore, we should be careful not to overestimate either because, as Boland reminds us, she is, first and foremost, 'a voice'.[35] Both 'In a Bad Light' and 'Love' from her 1994 collection *In a Time of Violence*, capture the concerns that drive Boland's exploration of displacement. 'In a Bad Light' recalls a visit to a St Louis museum:

> I stand in a room in the Museum.
>   In one glass case a plastic figure
> represents a woman in a dress,
>   with crêpe sleeves and a satin apron.
> And feet laced neatly into suede.[36]

The speaker learns that while 'the silk is French' ... the 'seamstresses are Irish': this knowledge sets off a chain of reflection, given that the women had emigrated from Ireland in the wake of the Famine and were now in St Louis near the outbreak of the Civil War. The museum's elegant display of this work by Irish women, the fact that their work is nowadays located in such a place and

Boland's sensitivity to their lives and labours draws the speaker into their world:

> I see them in the oil-lit parlours.
>   I am in the gas-lit backrooms.
> We make in the apron front and from
>   the papery appearance and crushable
> look of crêpe, a sign. We are bent over
>
>   in a bad light. We are sewing a last
> sight of shore. We are sewing coffin ships.
>   And the salt of exile. And our own
> death in it. For history's abandonment
>   we are doing this. And this ...[37]

For Boland, markers of these women's separation from Ireland are encoded in their work and visible to her because she has shared something of their experiences, albeit from another century and in different circumstances. By imaginatively involving herself in their tasks, Boland reminds herself that she too has been formed by exile. Like Seamus Heaney's famous 'Digging', Boland's 'In a Bad Light' is an example of an *ars poetica* in which the art of writing is aligned with manual craft. Both poets, in important democratic gestures, break down the barriers between high art and the art of the people.[38] In Boland's case, it is important to note that this gesture takes place in America before an exhibition of work by Irish American women. It is a poem written by an Irish American poet in a city of confluence, where things come together, 'This is St. Louis. Where the rivers meet./The Illinois. The Mississippi. The Missouri ...'[39]

'Love', as already mentioned, is set in Iowa City and recalls a period spent there when Boland was part of the University of Iowa's International Writing Program. It is a deeply personal poem recounting her daughter's illness with, and recovery from, meningitis. Here, the voice is that of mother, wife and poet and the allusions and tropes are not derived from, or pointed towards, exile but in the direction of classical literature, another important part of Boland's literary map. For the Irish person living abroad, many conditions of life are not the result of exile; rather, they occur because one has no choice and what transpires must be addressed out of love, necessity and fidelity.[40] Exile is not simple; in fact, sometimes exile is not even part of the equation when the process involves going back and forth to Ireland from other parts of the world. Boland understands the complexity of exile and her work gives elegant voice to its many-sidedness.

By choosing to use exile rather than emigration/immigration as her term of reference, Eavan Boland reminds her readers that estrangement and separation from Ireland remain potent parts of people's lives, even if absences from Ireland may well be temporary now. Technology, one of Boland's other interests, allows individuals to remain in touch with friends and family at home in real time though in virtual rather than substantive modes of engagement. In Boland's wide and organic view, Irish exiles across generations are linked by common experiences. She does not argue in her work that the Ryanair-Irish are exact replicas of the coffin-ship Irish – to do so would be ludicrous – but what she does point us towards are the elements of shared experience that are the result of dislocation and loss. On another level, Irish women and men are energized, liberated and re-educated by absence from Ireland, and able, like Eavan Boland, to bring back to Ireland new ways of thinking and expanded notions of how to live in this world. To be Irish and Irish American is not only possible, but it is also desirable and it is no bad thing to be guided by multiple attachments to place that are as deep as they are resource building – both for individuals and for the communities they belong to and serve. If today's Irish emigrants are in Bolger's view 'commuters', they are also women and men whose links to Ireland and elsewhere are not slight. The lives of Irish emigrants belong in our literature. Eavan Boland gives them a dignified voice. Of course Eavan Boland is an Irish American poet though she is also simultaneously a poet of other places and other times and spaces.

NOTES

1. Eavan Boland, *Object Lessons: The Life of a Woman and the Poet in Our Time* (Norton, 1995), p. 35.
2. Jody Allen Randolph, *Eavan Boland* (Bucknell University Press, 2014), pp 1–11.
3. Boland, *Object Lessons*, p. 37.
4. Dominic Sandbrook, *Never Had it So Good: A History of Britain from the Suez to the Beatles* (Abacus, 2006), p. 48.
5. Allen Randolph, pp 18–19.
6. Eavan Boland, 'An Irish Childhood in England: 1951', *New Collected Poems* (Norton, 2008), p. 93.
7. Boland, *Object Lessons*, p. 37.
8. Boland, *New Collected Poems*, pp 231–32.
9. Colm Tóibín, *Brooklyn* (Scribner, 2009), p. 46.
10. Tóibín, *Brooklyn*, pp 32–33.
11. Alistair Macleod, 'Vision', *Island: The Collected Stories* (Emblem Editions, 2001), p. 321.
12. Allen Randolph, p. xxi.
13. Boland, *Object Lessons*, p. 55.
14. Eavan Boland, *New Collected Poems*, p. 255.
15. Dermot Bolger (ed.) *Ireland in Exile: Irish Writers Abroad* (New Island Books, 1993), p. 7.
16. *Object Lessons*, p. 54.
17. *Ibid*, p. 53.
18. Allen Randolph, p. xxi.
19. John Montague, *The Rough Field* (Wake Forest University Press, 1989, 5th ed.).
20. Padraic Fiacc (ed.), *The Wearing of the Black* (Blackstaff Press, 1974).
21. Guinn Batten, '"Something Mourns": Wordsworth and the Landscape of Mourning in *The Rough Field* (1972)' in Thomas Dillon Redshaw (ed.), *Well Dreams: Essays on John Montague* (Creighton University Press, 2004), pp 167–193.
22. Gerald Dawe, 'Introduction' in Gerald Dawe and Aodán Mac Póilin (eds), *Ruined Pages: Selected Poems of Padraic Fiacc* (Blackstaff Press, 1994), p. 4.

23 'Our Father' in Gerald Dawe and Aodán Mac Póilin (eds), *Ruined Pages: Selected Poems of Padraic Fiacc* (Blackstaff Press, 1994), p. 93.
24 Frank McCourt, *Angela's Ashes* (Scribner, 1996).
25 Daniel Tobin, *The Book of Irish American Poetry: From the Eighteenth Century to the Present* (University of Notre Dame Press, 2007), pp 87–89.
26 Grace Schulman (ed.), *The Poems of Marianne Moore* (Viking, 2003), p. 246.
27 Allen Randolph, pp 1–11.
28 Allen Randolph, p. 55.
29 Eavan Boland, *In a Time of Violence* (Carcanet, 1994), p. 18.
30 Allen Randolph, p. 21.
31 Charles Fanning, *The Irish Voice in America* (University of Kentucky Press, 1990, 2000), p. 4.
32 Fanning, p. 368.
33 Daniel Tobin, *Awake in America: On Irish American Poetry* (University of Notre Dame Press, 2011), p. 11.
34 Boland, *New Collected Poems*, p. 204.
35 Boland, *Ibid*, p. 235.
36 Boland, *Ibid*, p. 207.
37 Boland, *Ibid*, pp 207–08.
38 Seamus Heaney, 'Digging', *Death of a Naturalist* (Faber, 1966), pp 1–2.
39 Boland, *New Collected Poems*, p. 207.
40 Boland, *Object Lessons*, p. 35.

REFERENCES

Boland, Eavan, *Domestic Violence* (Norton, 2007).
  In a Time of Violence (Norton, 1994).
  New Collected Poems (Norton, 2008).
  Object Lessons: The Life of a Woman and the Poet in Our Time (Norton, 1995).
  The Lost Land (Carcanet, 1998).
McCourt, Frank, *Angela's Ashes* (Scribner, 1996).
Stevens, Wallace, 'Our Stars Come from Ireland' and 'The Irish Cliffs of Moher' in Daniel Tobin (ed.), *The Book of Irish American Poetry: From the Eighteenth Century to the Present* (University of Notre Dame Press, 2007, pp 87–89).

Rory Gallagher's Blues

Rory Gallagher died, aged forty-seven, at London's King's College Hospital on 14 June 1995 at 10.44am from complications following a liver transplant. Although the transplant had been a success, and the patient was near the point in his recovery where his doctors were ready to move him from the transplant centre back to Cromwell Hospital, near his brother's and manager's home, two days before the anticipated transfer Gallagher caught a virus that, due to a ravaged immune system, he was unable to fight. It has been estimated that his funeral Mass and burial in Cork attracted 4000 mourners, many of whom had travelled from throughout Europe to be present; this large attendance included members of The Dubliners, U2, Martin Carthy and many of the musicians Gallagher had played with over the years.[1] His death was major news in Ireland, photographs from his funeral dominating the front pages of *The Cork Examiner*, *The Daily Mirror* and other newspapers. On 8 November a memorial Mass was held in London followed by a reception at the Irish Embassy attended by Bob Geldof, Van Morrison and others.[2] Ironically in 1941, in what must seem like a fable from another age, the Irish government under de Valera's leadership had refused to send a representation to James Joyce's funeral in Zurich – fifty years having lessened cultural anxieties.

Today, to celebrate his music and commemorate his life, Cork boasts a Rory Gallagher Place and Cork City Library has opened a Rory Gallagher Wing, while Paris claims a rue de Rory Gallagher. Since his brother's death, Donal Gallagher has overseen the re-mastering and re-issuing of Gallagher's back catalogue and these ranked second in sales in CDs reissued by BMG Music during the first quarter of the reissue programme.[3] Only Elvis Presley's back catalogue sold more during this period – a sure testament to the continued popularity of Gallagher's music among those who had witnessed his concerts, or owned his records on vinyl, or who had first discovered Gallagher's music in the years after he had passed away. Writing of Rory Gallagher, Diarmaid Ferriter noted that 'the influential music paper *Melody Maker* named Gallagher … the best guitarist in the world in the early 1970s'.[4]

In addition to paying tribute to his genius as a musician, songwriter and performer, my interest here is in recalling Gallagher's recordings and contexts and to trace his development as a musician, noting the importance of the grounding he received during his early years in Cork where he played in showbands and founded Taste, and his early forays to Belfast, at that time considered the epicentre of Irish rock 'n roll. To find the roots of his music and to better understand what he sought to achieve, I will explore what he learned, inherited and borrowed from the blues musicians and songwriters of the Delta and Chicago. The many connections between Ireland and America are widely understood; however, the blues does not always figure prominently in such discussions, and for this reason I am eager to remind readers of the great contributions made by Rory Gallagher to the musical traditions of both countries.

While we have always regarded the blues as being American, after examining Rory Gallagher's career we must also think of it as being imaginatively Irish. Also, always an avid music fan and concert goer, Rory Gallagher's late-December concerts at the National Stadium in Dublin in the 1970s were for me rites of passage into this magical world of live musical performance that to this day remain the benchmarks by which I gauge the quality of concerts. These gigs also belong to another important phase in my own life – my introduction to the adult world. To recall Rory Gallagher's performances provides an opportunity for me to travel back across the decades to encounter my own youthful, immature and hopeful self. At nineteen, I was newly-liberated from boarding school, where nothing happened, and eager to engage with a world where anything might be possible.

A few years before my first visit to the stadium to hear Gallagher in concert, Marcus Connaughton had had his own first experience at the same venue while Gallagher was leading Taste:

> The first time I saw Rory Gallagher play was with the second line-up of Taste – John Wilson on drums and Richie McCracken on bass guitar – in the National Boxing Stadium on the South Circular Road in Dublin in 1968. I bumped into Rory in the gent's toilet, which was a fairly primitive affair in the Stadium, and like many young fans (I was sixteen) it was an amazing thing to meet your hero. As ever, Rory was an absolute gentleman and nodded and wished well to myself and my friend Eddie Breslin ...[5]

Nowadays settled in Gallagher's native Cork, Connaughton leads Rory Gallagher walking tours in the city. His 2014 book, *Rory Gallagher: His Life and Times*, is a splendid and informative guide to Gallagher's world, in many instances providing fan tidbits from behind the stories. For example, it is a well-known legend that Gallagher acquired his famous Fender Stratocaster guitar from Crowley's Music Centre on Cork's Merchant's Quay –

a subsequent visit to the store is featured in the documentary *Rory Gallagher: Irish Tour 1974* – but what is both strange and fascinating is Connaughton's account of the instrument's provenance:

> Michael Crowley had sold only two Strats prior to Rory showing an interest in the guitar. The first had gone to Jim Conlon of the Royal Showband in Waterford. Conlon liked the guitar but had to return it when the Royal Showband decided to change their uniforms. The sunburst Strat did not match the new salmon-pink colours of the band, and so it was sent back to the music store in Cork, travelling up from Waterford as cargo in the back of a bus. Michael Crowley had promised Rory's mother that he would let her know if he ever got a second-hand Strat, and so he went straight up to their home on Mac Curtain Street. 'I think that was around twelve o'clock in the morning. When we reopened at two, Rory was there, standing at the door. He came and looked at the guitar. I offered it to him and he just held it in his hand and said, "Yeah, that's it!" and ran off home'.[6]

Widely photographed, Gallagher's battered Strat would become instantly recognisable and even iconic to many music fans worldwide.

Growing up in the 1960s at the height of the Showband Era, I followed the fortunes of the Royal Showband, The Dixies, Joe Dolan and the Drifters and others, though I was then too young for nightlife and dancehalls. The showbands were coated in a certain degree of glamour and wildly popular though they did not capture my interest to the same extent as the singers and musicians comprising the 'Ballad Boom' had. Many Wexford people at the time disapproved of the raffish Dubliners, this attitude driving me into their embrace. Listening to the old people talking I took note of two aspects of Ronnie Drew's demeanour that they found objectionable: not only did he sport a 'dirty' beard but he also spoke with a 'thick Dublin accent'. One of my relatives condemned him as a communist. The blues was not on my childhood radar, though the new musical styles emerging from England were. I recall one day seeing a young man clad in a pair of pointed shoes walk across the Market Square and so spellbound was I by his footwear that I followed him over the bridge and up Shannon Hill. For most of my generation growing up in Enniscorthy, entertainment centred on the Astor Cinema and St Aidan's Cathedral with the dull routine being broken on occasion by visits to Leinster finals in Croke Park.

Later on, when I was sent there, boarding school seemed a total wash-out, run by monks who appeared to labour under the illusion that it was still 1300. Rory Gallagher was an antidote to both the showband scene and to the dullness and claustrophobia of the times: he wore a flannel shirt and jeans rather than a salmon-pink suit; he rocked his audience into a frenzy of excitement rather than creating an artificial environment punctuated by alternating slow and fast sets; and he shook his audiences out of inherited lethargies. At that time, Ireland was still ideologically rural whereas Gallagher's music was urban. Elvis might have been king; however, for us, dismal old Dev was still president and, depending on one's opinion, the best of a bad lot. We were all praying for the old patriots to die off. Soon, this would come to pass, though events in the north would, simultaneously, push other backward cadres into the limelight. Marcus Connaughton's book is also a splendid guide to the Cork of Gallagher's youth, particularly in relation to the minutiae of its music scene – where records could be purchased, who played where and when, for example.

Prophetically, Rory Gallagher was born in the Rock Hospital in Ballyshannon, County Donegal, on 2 March 1948 and later christened at the Rock Church. His father was a musician and Gallagher was given his first guitar when he was eight years old, after the family had moved to Cork, his mother's birthplace. All accounts of Gallagher's development as a musician point to the enduring support he received from his mother. Quickly, he mastered his instrument and his repertoire progressed from the ballads and traditional music so beloved of his mother to the skiffle of Lonnie Donegan, who was Gallagher's musical idol as a child. Gallagher was also in the process of discovering the music of Elvis Presley, Eddie Cochran, Buddy Holly, Gene Vincent and Chuck Berry. By this time, Gallagher was already playing professionally with The Fontana, an outfit, according to Colin Harper and Trevor Hodgett, that was one small part of the frenetic showband entertainment machine of the era:

> At its peak, there were said to be around six hundred matching-suited acts shuttling up and down the island, packing them in on a vast circuit of rural ballrooms (fourteen of which were owned by future Irish prime minister Albert Reynolds) with grueling five-hour shows encompassing UK chart covers, comedy, Elvis and Jim Reeves ... In joining The Fontana [Showband], later updating its name to The Impact, Rory was simply one of many creative souls obliged to learn their craft in a mohair suit.[7]

According to his fellow Irish guitarist and contemporary Henry McCullough, Gallagher was the first of the showband musicians to successfully make the break from the showband circuit to the beat scene. This was achieved when he founded Taste, originally called The Taste, with bassist Eric Kitteringham and drummer Norman D'Amery, in Cork in 1966.[8] This was the beginning of a journey that would culminate in Gallagher being labelled 'The First Irish Rock Star'. He set out to write, play and record his own compositions and the blues of the Delta and Chicago. At that time, Belfast was the centre of the Irish R&B scene and Taste arrived there in early 1967 to play such venues as the Maritime Hotel, which had acquired legendary status as the venue where Van Morrison and Them had played before becoming famous, and were taken under the wing of Eddie Kennedy, a former ballroom dancer who booked bands for the Maritime. Speaking of the vibrant Belfast scene of that time, Van Morrison noted:

> Memphis Slim had been in Belfast; Jesse Fuller, Champion Jack Dupree, John Lee Hooker's been there. They got folk clubs and rock clubs there, but it's got nothing to do with the English scene. In fact, I'd go so far as to say it doesn't have much to do with [the] Irish scene either, it's just Belfast. It's got its own identity, it's got its own people ... it's just a different race, a different breed of people. There's a lot of changes there, too. Like the McPeakes on one hand, and some others of us on the other hand, and they're open to all kinds of music, not just one thing. Maybe a third of the kind of people that are into R&B would go to hear the McPeakes.[9]

It seems likely that the openness which Morrison refers to was liberating both for himself and for Gallagher, both musicians and songwriters who were interested in exploring various musical genres under the rock 'n roll umbrella. Going to Belfast took Taste away from a showband-dominated world and into a space where their own music could be better understood and where they would likely grow as musicians and performers. At the same time, as Connaughton points out, Cork was hardly the backwater it might have appeared with acts such as John Mayall and his Bluesbreakers playing there in 1966 for example.[10] For Gallagher, Belfast represented a first foothold in a larger musical world and it was equally important, as Van Morrison points out, that it was an open city willing to accept innovation, as Hamburg had been in earlier decades. Its beat scene transcended the city's religious and economic divides. A musical tradition like the blues, rooted in exploitation, poverty and slavery could hardly be used as an instrument of sectarianism. Like socialist belief, the blues and beat music in general served as an antidote to sectarianism and a way of transcending a divided place. Also, the blues was the music of another place – the American south primarily – an unlikely space on whose cultural shoulders a synthesis could be forged.

Writing of this period in Britain, the music critic Charles Shaar Murray believed that:

> the spiritual and geographical distance which separated Brit bands from their sources ultimately proved to be their greatest asset. Lacking first-hand knowledge of and access to their role models, they were forced to reinvent the music, to juxtapose styles and idioms which rarely mixed on their native soil.[11]

Belfast blues was marked by its own particular *blas*. Both Gallagher and Van Morrison present visions of benign masculinity, though the experiences which ground their work are less harrowing than those which underlined the lives of their musical masters, as LeRoi Jones illustrates in his study of African American music: 'A slave cannot be a man. A man does not, or is not supposed to, work all of his life without recourse to the other means of human existence'.[12] Even though Irish and African American experiences are quite different, they can be connected by legacies of displacement, punishment, want and, by the way, both Irish and African Americans were considered to be inferior by their 'betters'. Modern Irish and African American blues are written at a remove from the Irish Famine and from American slavery; however, this is part of how the music has been conceived, as Titon points out:

> The blues was conceived by freedmen and ex-slaves – if not as a result of a personal or intellectual experience, at least as an emotional confirmation of, and reaction to, the way in which most Negroes were still forced to exist in the United States.[13]

In both the blues and Irish traditional music and song, the experiences of the past are brought into the present in melody and lyric with discrete locations providing particular nuances and styles from Memphis to Belfast.

In May 1968, Eddie Kennedy took Taste to England where they quickly secured gigs backing such well-known performers as Captain Beefheart and playing guest spots on John Peel's *Top Gear* – until Peel's death the most influential source for new music in the UK. Eventually, after

Kitteringham and D'Amery were replaced by Richard 'Charlie' McCracken and John Wilson, Taste recorded two albums, *Taste* (1969) and *On the Boards* (1970); the former selling over two hundred thousand copies in the first year after its release.[14] In a short period the band became enormously successful – they played throughout Europe and North America, where they toured in support of Blind Faith, supported Cream at their farewell Albert Hall concert and played at the 1970 Isle of Wight Festival alongside The Doors, The Who, Joni Mitchell, Jimi Hendrix, Miles Davis among others. In hindsight, one can see Taste's and Gallagher's presence at this festival (he was barely twenty-two years of age) as a landmark. First, the emergence of Van Morrison and, second, the arrival of Gallagher had emphasised that the Irish would have a role to play in the shaping of modern rock 'n roll.[15] For up-and-coming musicians in Ireland, particularly in the Republic, present and future, Gallagher's success secured permission, to borrow Eavan Boland's term, for them to find their paths in music.[16]

After the Isle of Wight Festival, Gallagher disbanded Taste to embark on a solo career. According to Harper and Hodgett, 'Taste were the victims of their own rapid success and inexperience. Eddie Kennedy had steered them from a fiver to £2000 a night in two years'.[17] For a long time after the break-up of Taste, the Gallagher brothers sought to recover lost earnings – first from Kennedy himself and later from his estate. Their final concert was played at Queen's University, Belfast on 31 December 1970, as part of a tour that took place purely to satisfy contractual agreements. According to Coghe, Gallagher was blamed for the split and viewed as someone who, as a consequence of success, had become a dictator. One result of this acrimony was his refusal to play Taste songs for years afterwards.[18] Marcus Connaughton's account of the split is more nuanced with drummer John Wilson concluding that 'if the business had been handled in a different way then it may never have led to the break-up of something so special'.[19]

As a soloist, Gallagher recorded fourteen albums between 1971 and 1990. In addition he played on recordings by such artists as Muddy Waters, Jerry Lee Lewis, Lonnie Donegan, Davy Spillane, The Furey Brothers & Davy Arthur, Stiff Little Fingers, The Dubliners, Peter Green and the Rolling Stones (on 'Miss You'), who sought him out as a potential replacement for Mick Taylor.[20] It is ironic that even though Gallagher's most important work was composed after he had disbanded Taste, he would face an uphill struggle to capture the imagination and support of music fans that he had enjoyed around the time of the Isle of Wight festival. Gerry Smyth believes that Gallagher's 'music and image stalled ... around 1970' though I would argue that it was the reception that had stalled rather than the music itself.[21] When we evaluate popular music and other artistic endeavours, we are inclined to assume that commercial sales and artistic success are part of a continuum, whereas this does not reflect hard reality. In popular music in particular, large-scale success is frequently short-lived and, often, it has been the case that the best music has been composed and played far beneath the radar of the charts. To dismiss Gallagher's solo career as Smyth does is unfair. Richard Thompson's contributions to music – like Gallagher's – could be discounted for the same reason. Equally, in other artistic endeavours such as writing, sales are not always the best benchmark of quality, with the bestseller lists often dominated by dross and effluent.

Taste emerged at the height of the British blues explosion and, like Cream, who were the dominant figures in this movement, successfully wedded Delta and Chicago blues with British blues-rock, as Smyth points out:

> The form was organized around two central elements: the traditional, three-cord blues song and an instrumental ability to improvise at length around the basic chordal structure. The

electrification of instruments owed much to the advent of rock 'n roll, and the idea of a long, semi-improvised solo was clearly borrowed from the jazz tradition ...[22]

The break-up of Cream marked the end of the blues explosion – from this point onward other forms and variations would become more popular and the three-piece blues ensemble would seem constricting and somewhat out-of-step with the new aesthetics and a more 'modern' *zeitgeist*. Many of the guitarists who had popularised the blues in England – Eric Clapton, Jimmy Page, Alvin Lee, Mick Taylor – would abandon the three-piece unit and progress to play in a variety of bands and across musical genres. Of the great players of this period only Gallagher and Jeff Beck remained rooted in tradition – at various levels, and over time, and despite their artistic accomplishments, they would become more marginal figures. However, Smyth's conclusions are more relative than they are fixed and final. Throughout the 1970s, given Gallagher's recordings and his hectic touring schedule, one could hardly have claimed that he was a marginal figure, except in America where, despite many tours, he never succeeded in reaching a large audience. Eventually, to expand musical possibilities, he would add a keyboardist to his band and, later on, a harmonica player. Connaughton highlights Gallagher's popularity on the European mainland so, while he had lost a certain degree of popularity in the UK as a result of changing tastes, his music remained in vogue elsewhere. Of course, the emergence of punk marginalised certain types of music, including Gallagher's, though this is ironic given Gallagher's credibility and his flannel-shirt image or anti-image. He was always an iconoclast and outsider and the antithesis of glam rock. But the tide was impossible to fight.

Gallagher's first solo recording, *Rory Gallagher*, was released in 1971 and featured a second Belfast rhythm section – Gerry McAvoy on bass and Wilgar Campbell on drums – with Vincent Crane of Atomic Rooster guesting on piano. Harper and Hodgett write of the album that it:

> is a beautiful, subtle album of virtually end-to-end highlights. It stands alongside Jethro Tull's *Aqualung* and with Led Zeppelin *III* as one of the year's defining moments ... Not quite as macho as Zeppelin, nor a willfully quirky as Tull, Gallagher had created his own sound, drawing from modern jazz chordings and octave soloing, urban and delta blues, straight-ahead rock and Celtic folk.[23]

Recalling the making of the album, Gallagher recalled that:

> it had a nice atmosphere ... Not as hard or rocky as some of the Taste stuff, nor the later recordings either. A little tight sound – all live vocals and live lead guitar. Recorded very quietly with one little Fender amp and a twelve-inch speaker.[24]

In addition to the influence of the blues, the album illustrates the degree to which Gallagher had steeped himself in jazz and folk music. It was through his immersion in the work of Django Reinhardt, Ornette Coleman, John Coltrane and his friendship with Don Van Vliet, better known as Captain Beefheart, that Gallagher was led to 'give freer rein [to] his creative process'.[25] From playing in showbands, Gallagher had learned the operational etiquette of 'unbending musical discipline where nothing was left to chance' though this was eventually superceded by lessons learned from jazz.[26] While living in a bedsit in London in 1967, he had learned to play the saxophone from books, records and from setting himself the task of learning a tune each day. So as not to annoy his landlord, Gallagher practiced in the room's only wardrobe.[27]

Of course, it for his live performances that Gallagher is most often remembered. According to Fairport Convention's Dave Pegg, 'he really knew how to manage a crowd'.[28] Harper and Hodgett note:

> Most people's recollection of Rory Gallagher today is of a lean, frenetic figure storm-trooping around festival and city hall

stages all through the Seventies with a permanent checked shirt and archetypal battered Strat, flanked on one side by Gerry McAvoy, splay-legged, head-banging and writing the text book for the pummeling school of bass guitar. Rory's live shows were high-energy affairs. 'It would start with the encore – that's what it was like,' says Dino McGartland. 'We'd go home shattered.' Any number of *Old Grey Whistle Test* specials [on BBC], or his record number of *Rockpalast* broadcasts on German TV, bear this out.[29]

Gallagher toured tirelessly and worldwide. His Irish concerts during the 1970s are particularly important, occurring at a time before Ireland featured on the map for well-known recording artists, due to The Troubles. For many young Irish music fans, myself included, a Rory Gallagher concert represented a rare opportunity to witness a performance by a major international artist in Ireland. In addition, Gallagher was alone among first-rank performers who consistently played in the north throughout the Troubles, as is noted by everyone who has written on popular music in Ireland. One can be certain that his high-energy and no-frills attitude and mien influenced such bands as Stiff Little Fingers, with whom Gallagher subsequently recorded, and the Undertones who would emerge in the late-Seventies as part of the Punk-New Wave phenomenon.

As previously noted, Gallagher's decision to forego a radical change in musical direction meant that he had set himself the task of working within the narrower confines of a musical genre that had begun to recede from popularity. Of course, he himself would hardly have seen his future in this way; instead, he might have commented on the degree of continuity that had existed in his career from the first instant he'd heard the blues – that long moment that set him on his life's path. In this respect it is clear that to understand his aesthetic and achievement, Gallagher's work is best discussed in the context of the blues of the Delta and Chicago. Giles Oakley has defined the blues in this way:

> The principal theme of the country blues, and probably of all blues, is the sexual relationship. Almost all other themes, leaving town, train rides, work trouble, general dissatisfaction sooner or later revert to the central concern. Most frequently the core of the relationship is seen as inherently unstable, transient, but with infinite scope for pleasure and exultation in success, or pain and torment in failure. This gives the blues its tension and ambiguity, dealing simultaneously with togetherness and loneliness, communion and isolation, physical joy and emotional anguish. In Patton's blues, even the sound itself has the feeling of tension, with damped down, 'dirty' toned, monotonously repeated bass figures giving a heavy emotional undertow, lightened by the sensuously rising and sliding notes, driving and swinging with the joy of release.[30]

In addition to writing his own songs under the influence of his American predecessors, Gallagher performed, recorded, rearranged and imitated the works of the masters: Charley Patton, Robert Johnson, Muddy Waters, Blind Boy Fuller and many others. It was in their footsteps he walked, to their tradition he owed allegiance, and his achievement resides alongside theirs. Gallagher's songs are full of the themes that Oakley enumerates and based on the structures and techniques that passed from Clarksdale to Chicago to Cork. Even though the blues had emerged from the American south rooted in the lives of the dispossessed and the particular conditions of *their* dispossession, African American at its roots and core, it contained elements, or archetypes, that would give it wide appeal beyond its various borders for, as Little Brother Montgomery has said, 'blues come from within, the music come from within a person, it don't come out of a conservatory'.[31] In a 1993 interview, John Lee Hooker when asked about the music of Robert Johnson concluded that:

it could be any country or any state, and over the years, I guess it would be. Nowadays, he could be any state or any country. But then, that was the kind of music in the South.[32]

In Ralph Ellison's opinion the blues is 'an autobiographical chronicle of catastrophe, expressed lyrically' and this would seem to indicate that it is available to all.[33] In this respect, one is tempted to suppose that Rory Gallagher's facility with the blues is rooted in his own cultural inheritance as an Irishman – one of the dispossessed, rejected, defeated, evicted, lampooned and exiled. We might argue perhaps that Gallagher's blues is Ireland's blues. But to take this path might be reductive. Even though Gallagher enjoyed a rather unremarkable Irish childhood and was exposed to life, culture, history, tradition, music and religion in the same manner as others growing up in the decades after 'The Emergency', he remade himself imaginatively to become a bluesman. To draw strident parallels between the experience of the Irish in Ireland and African Americans in the south, while superficially attractive and supported on some levels by fact, is to invite specious generalisation and to assume that Irish people have the inside track when it comes to understanding the African American experience. In his book, *Searching for Robert Johnson*, Peter Guralnick reaches the following conclusion of Johnson's achievement and I would like to think that we can apply his summary to Rory Gallagher's:

> Robert Johnson became the personification of the existential blues singer, unencumbered by corporeality or history, a fiercely incandescent spirit who had escaped the bonds of tradition by the sheer trust of genius.[34]

We can also apply Muddy Waters' accounting of his own achievement to Gallagher's – '[I] took the old-time music and brought it up to date'.[35] Gallagher, an intensely-shy man, found in the blues the objective correlative for his talent, skill, imagination and feeling. He fits a mold described by his fellow Corkonian Frank O'Connor who noted that 'writers who come from Catholic Ireland do bring with them something of its anonymity, [and they] are more impersonal, more identified with their material'.[36]

Lyrically, there seems little that is of his direct life in Gallagher's work; rather, the weight of passion and personality is conveyed more subtly and indirectly. The on-stage and off-stage Gallaghers can appear to be radically-different persons, though this is not unusual among creative people. The final years of Gallagher's life, when he had passed his peak in popularity and his health had begun to deteriorate, were difficult. It was then that he came to understand what he had forfeited – a private life and a family – to live the life of a touring musician. He was consumed by efforts to win back his back catalogue, grew obsessed with astrology and superstition, abandoned his checked shirt for a more somber black one, was 'racked with self-doubt', most inopportunely, at a time when a blues revival was taking place, and was often over-medicated.[37] At the same time, his late recordings – *Defender* (1987) and *Fresh Evidence* (1990) – are considered by many to be among his best. His final years were spent at the Conrad Hotel in London close by a house he owned in Earl's Court in which he had never lived. He became a Howard Hughes-like figure dying at forty-seven, the same age as F. Scott Fitzgerald when he died, both great artists who reached the heights of fame while young, were quickly forgotten and then rehabilitated to the pantheon after their deaths, with the former's facilitated by the advent of the CD, the latter's by the advent of the paperback.

This is how Francis Davis describes a central journey in the history of the blues:

> In Clarksdale, Mississippi, one Friday afternoon in May 1943, a twenty-eight-year-old tractor driver on Stovall's Farms who had somehow eluded the draft caught the 4:00pm train to Memphis. Carrying only his guitar (mail-ordered from Sears,

Roebuck for $11) and a suitcase with one change of clothes, McKinley Morganfield – nicknamed 'Muddy Waters' from his childhood in Rolling Fork, Mississippi – switched trains in Memphis, boarding a northbound Illinois Central and taking it to Chicago, the end of the line.[38]

In his life, in his own time and in his own way, Rory Gallagher left Cork for Belfast, which was his own Chicago. On the one hand a musical genius, on the other just another player setting out on the long, hard road plied by all musicians. For me, not once in a million years as I listened to Rory Gallagher's music as a teenager did I ever think it possible that I might visit Clarksdale. But today, following Highway 61 home on our return from a visit to our daughter and her husband in Louisiana, my wife Drucilla and I have rolled into town. I have parked the car. And I am remembering Rory Gallagher of Cork as I walk through Clarksdale. I have died and gone to heaven.

NOTES

1. Jean-Noël Coghe, *Rory Gallagher: A Biography*, translated by Lorna Carson and Brian Steer (Mercier Press, 2005), pp 168–77.
2. *Ibid*, p. 179.
3. Colin Harper and Trevor Hodgett, *Irish Folk, Trad and Blues* (Collins Press, 2004), p. 222.
4. Diarmaid Ferriter, *Ambiguous Republic: Ireland in the 1970s* (Profile Books, 2012), p. 270.
5. Marcus Connaughton, *Rory Gallagher: His Life and Times* (Collins Press, 2014), p. 34.
6. Connaughton, p. 3.
7. Harper and Hodgett, p. 226.
8. Harper, p. 227.
9. Gerald Dawe, *In Another World: Van Morrison and Belfast* (Merrion Press, 2017), pp 40–41.
10. Connaughton, p. 13.
11. Roberta Freund Schwartz, 'Putting the Blues in British Blues Rock' in Jill Terry and Neil A. Wynn (eds), *Transatlantic Roots Music: Folk, Blues, and National Identities* (University of Mississippi Press, 2012), p. 147.

12 LeRoi Jones, *Blues People: The Negro Experience in White America and the Music that Developed from It* (William Morrow, 1963), p. 60.
13 Jeff Todd Titon, *Early Downhome Blues: A Musical and Cultural Analysis* (University of North Carolina Press, 1994), 2nd ed, p. 142.
14 Connaughton, p. 35.
15 Coghe, pp 48–51.
16 Eavan Boland, *Object Lessons: The Life of the Woman and the Poet in Our Time* (Norton, 1995), p. xii.
17 Harper and Hodgett, p. 230.
18 Coghe, p. 51.
19 Connaughton, p. 49.
20 Harper, p. 233.
21 Gerry Smyth, *Noisy Island: A Short History of Irish Popular Music* (Cork University Press, 2005), pp 36–7.
22 *Ibid*, p. 36.
23 Harper and Hodgett, p. 223.
24 Harper, *Ibid*, p. 233.
25 Coghe, p. 41.
26 *Ibid*.
27 *Ibid*.
28 Harper, p. 232.
29 Harper and Hodgett, p. 232.
30 Giles Oakley, *The Devil's Music: A History of the Blues* (Da Capo Press, 1997), p. 55.
31 Oakley, p. 42.
32 Francis Davis, *The History of the Blues* (Hyperion, 1995), p. 53.
33 Davis, p. 243.
34 Peter Guralnick, *Searching for Robert Johnson* (Dutton, 1989), p. 2.
35 Davis, p. 175.
36 Frank O'Connor, 'The Future of Irish Literature' in David Pierce (ed.), *Irish Writing in the Twentieth Century: A Reader* (Cork University Press, 2000), p. 501.
37 Harper, p. 237.
38 Davis, p. 175.

REFERENCES

Frith, Simon, 'The Cultural Study of Popular Music' in Lawrence Grossberg, Cary Nelson, Paula A. Treichler (eds), *Cultural Studies* (Routledge, 1992, pp 174–182).

Gallagher, Rory, *Rory Gallagher* (BMG, 1971, 1999).
  Live in Europe (BMG, 1972, 1999).

Oliver, Paul, Tony Russell, Robert M. W. Dixon, John Godrich, and Howard Rye, *Yonder Come the Blues: The Evolution of a Genre* (Cambridge University Press, 2001).

Palmer, Tony, *Rory Gallagher Irish Tour 1974* (BMG, 2000).

Taste, *On the Boards* (Polydor, 1970, 1994).

Wardlow, Gayle Dean, *Chasin' That Devil Music: Searching for the Blues*, Edward Komara (ed.) (San Francisco, 1998).

THE USE OF MEMORY:
MICHAEL COADY'S *ALL SOULS*

Published in 1997, *All Souls,* Michael Coady's third collection of poetry, was one of that year's best received volumes of new work. It is a rich, varied, eclectic and inspired compendium that incorporates poetry, story, illustration and memoir to reflect the interlocking and overlapping territories of peoples and places and time and memory across Ireland and America. The work is ambitious in scope, theme and design, embracing poetic and colloquial voices, the Irish and English languages, the often painful experiences of the Irish diaspora and the residual experiences of loss felt by those who remained in Ireland. *All Souls* is also an exploration of the poet's family history, which thematically and emotionally frames the work and it is shaped, though hardly bordered, by Carrick-on-Suir, County Tipperary, where Coady has lived his life as writer and teacher, and by the experiences of the emigrant Coadys in the United States. *All Souls* is a literary work of the highest order, an individual act of recovery of family history and, on a larger level, a representation of the pained mechanics of exile. In modern Irish poetry the works it most closely resemble are John Montague's *The Dead Kingdom* and Ciaran Carson's *Belfast Confetti*, both formally ambitious poetic expressions of history and place, though *All Souls*, in its odyssey of styles, can perhaps be best compared to James Joyce's *Ulysses*. However, of the Irish poets of his own generation, Coady is thematically closest to Eavan Boland, a writer who, in both her poetry and prose, has made the diaspora a central platform of her work.

Writing of *All Souls*, Ciaran Carson notes that it:

> is a compendium of the implications of that family history, written like a symphony ... Few books like *All Souls* are being written these days, but I would like to think that such a book could only have come out of Ireland: it unites the demotic and the sophisticated; it speaks through the mouths of people, and encompasses all kinds of art. Society and destiny shape us, but we shape them.[1]

Theo Dorgan writes that:

> in his new collection Michael Coady stands quietly but firmly before us as a man gifted with true humility, committed to the stringent duties of memory, memorialist to a place and to a people. It is a remarkably human and unillusioned book, a work of scruple and playfulness, astringent, elegiac and true.[2]

In *The Irish Times*, Caitriona O'Reilly noted that *All Souls* defies accurate classification and:

> comprises biographical prose, epigram, lyric verse, and translations from the Irish, all executed with considerable generosity and vivacity ... [and] charged with feeling and vivid detail while skillfully avoiding sentiment or nostalgia.[3]

Looking back over Coady's published work, it is clear that *All Souls* is also a work of artistic culmination where recovery is brought into sharper focus and where themes that had once been explored in short lyrics are now developed on a larger scale and in a variety of forms. In his first collection, *Two for a Woman, Three for a Man*, which received the Patrick Kavanagh Award in 1979, many poems explore the ordinariness of small-town life in Carrick-on-Suir with particular reference to individuals whose time on earth has not been recorded, neither in history nor literature. In the title poem, the poet's brother, who is an emigrant and part of a class, in Coady's view, that has been written out of history, is quoted at their father's funeral:

> When the bell boomed three
> over my father's coffin
> my emigrant brother pale
> above his black tie shuddered
> *I couldn't live
> under that sound.*[4]

In 'Still Life from a Hill over a Town', the famine dead are recalled from history by the eerie specter of a key hanging on the wall of the poet's study:

> My wife and child are in a house
> Out on the edge of the frame;
> The key of the Workhouse which once
> Stood on the site
> Hangs on the wall of my study.[5]

In this early poem we are presented with an insight into Coady's *ars poetica*. The speaker is looking down over Carrick-on-Suir from a nearby hill composing a photograph in the viewer before pressing the shutter. In addition to presenting the physical complexity of the town and the river where 'Boys are fishing from a bridge/Built before Columbus raised a sail,' the photograph, because houses, shops and streets are repositories of the worlds of the living and dead, will contain resonant echoes of an unseen world that throbs within the frame's complex interior:

> Things I can't see are happening now
> Because they've always happened.
>
> An old man is dying,
> Girls are dressing for a wedding,
> A coffin is being prepared.

Under some roof
A man and woman
Are making love.[6]

Poetry, for Coady, must be equally in touch with present and past time, with town and country, with hill and street, with the river and the sea into which it flows and with the living voices of now and those that whisper back across centuries. For both Coady and Joyce, the town and city are both the microcosms of the world and the world itself. Though just thirty-two lines, 'Still Life from a Hill over a Town', is an ambitious and widely ranging poem and one that anticipates *All Souls*, published seventeen years later. Furthermore, throughout the period he has published poetry, Coady has also shown his photographs, both inside and on the covers of his books and it is clear that the process of composition moves fluidly from one artform to the next: one influences the other and vice versa. The best examples of Coady's photographs are to be found in *Full Tide*, a miscellany of prose articles, originally published in the Clonmel *Nationalist* for the most part, which appeared in 1999. These photographs record aspects of Carrick's public life – boys and men fishing on the Suir and the town's religious statuary – though Coady also includes the work of other photographers in *Full Tide* and a variety of visual images, a movie poster, sheet music for example, to indicate his desire to have his published work contain the three primary artistic activities of his life: poetry, photography and the music he has played and performed in public since childhood. Coady's use of collage in *Full Tide* and *All Souls* is one of the most important exercises of this kind by an Irish poet in recent times and comparable to John Montague's similar usage in *The Rough Field*. For both poets, the visual image, whether woodcut or photograph, or even the page's white space, is inseparable from the printed words of the poem.

In addition to marking out the road ahead, Coady's early work suggests a thematic kinship with the work of Eavan Boland, another poet concerned with mapping the lives of those erased from the narrative of history. Both poets reach backward into history from the known present to seek the silenced voices of the past and both use family history as their method of entry. In his first collection Coady is connected to emigration by the presence of his 'pale brother' at their father's funeral.[7] Boland's experience is first-hand when she is wrenched from Dublin as a child and brought to live in London:

> Long ago
> I was a child in a strange country:
>
> I was Irish in England.
>
> I learned
> a second language there
> which has stood me in good stead:
>
> The lingua franca of a lost land.[8]

It is a measure of Coady's capacity for empathy that he is able to so fully bring to life the emigrant experience in his work. His only recorded personal experience of emigration is found in 'Dreamland', an essay which details a summer of work in England when he was a student:

> I was a relatively innocent and shy young man never before out of Ireland. The loneliness of my first few weeks took me totally by surprise. I was ambushed by that unconsidered and unspoken thirst for the familiar and the ordinary that we call homesickness. Any Irish accent overheard on the street was refreshment and reassurance: a saving straw to clutch at.[9]

Coincidentally, both Coady and Boland are connected by Tipperary workhouses: the key of the old Carrick-on-Suir workhouse hangs on the wall of Coady's study while Boland, in her search though family history, locates her great-grandfather in the 1870s when he became master of the Clonmel Union (the workhouse's official title), situated a few miles upstream on the Suir from Carrick. In Coady's and in Boland's hands, as Daniel Tobin has pointed out, 'genealogy becomes a compelling tool of the imagination'.[10] Equally, their work, though very often very different in manner and enthusiasms, reaches back in time, to the nineteenth and early twentieth centuries in particular, to recover the forgotten, desperate, starving and diseased: the Irish who became lost.

At the beginning of *Oven Lane*, his second collection, Coady proclaims that he loves 'the abandon of abandoned things', a statement that sets the intent, if not the tone of the collection.[11] This phrase recalls the work of Derek Mahon, another poet enthralled by forsaken places and objects, though whereas for Mahon, in such poems as 'A Disused Shed in Co. Wexford', these explorations are philosophical in intent and ultimately explorations of disjunction, for Coady they are familial and modes of binding. Coady comes to the past to record the facts and the spirits of his own ancestry, his most tangible knot to history:

> A hundred years and I will come
> to try the lane for echoes
>
> the coughing and the crying
> of children in the dark,
> the nameless incarnations
> of love and grief and hunger
> where the river flows
> coldly past.[12]

Other poems in *Oven Lane*, literally the lane in Carrick leading to the river where generations of Coadys were raised, also look forward to *All Souls*. 'The Letter' presents the central narrative of *All Souls* in miniature: a poem in five sections rather than a book-length poetic symphony and which will be reprinted as the opening to the seventh section of *All Souls*. In addition Coady includes work that records time visiting the eastern United States, his interest in developing ties with his relatives there and his sense of kinship with the dead American Coadys, such as the Uncle Jim he had heard about but never met:

> In Easthampton cemetery
> I breathe for him a litany
> of distant names of places
> only he and I would know.[13]

In addition to many poems of observation of Carrick life linking the volume to *Two for a Woman, Three for a Man*, Coady includes 'Stopping by a Clare Graveyard After Hours', his formal elegy to the famous Clare musician and his great friend, Pakie Russell. Pakie and Micho Russell embody the connectedness that Coady finds essential to art:

> I know you were always a man
>   with a heart for the true thing,
> For a child or a saying, a woman,
>   a flower or a song,
> Life that came dancing through fingers
>   was most of your praying
> And your darkness redeemed in the shape
>   and surprise of the word.[14]

In the stanza's hierarchy, contact with people precedes the creation of art. It is out of such intense contacts, allied with the free interplay between the physical landscape and the poet and even with the dialogue between the living and dead, that true music and true poetry is made. To play music, dance and write poetry are activities as natural to humans as breathing:

> The tiding old sea is still taking
>   and giving and shaping,
> Gentians and violets break
>   in the spring from the stone,
> The world and its mother go reeling
>   and jigging forever
> In answer to something that troubles
>   the blood and the bone.[15]

Coady further recounts his relationship with the Russells in *The Well of Spring Water*, a prose work from 1996. In addition to immersing him in traditional music, the brothers introduced Coady to the vibrant oral culture of north Clare and reminded him of how songs and tunes are in continuous states of transmission and transformation as they pass from singer to singer and musician to musician. Each new version incorporates elements left by each singer and player, even if the performer is someone from outside the locale or tradition:

> The process of voluntary exploration and reconnection with the ancestral music tradition need not imply any kind of exclusivist stance. Different musical idioms should be able to co-exist in a context of mutually enriching esteem.[16]

Each contribution, if its intent is honest, is valuable. In Doolin and its environs, Coady can easily locate the vibrant Gaelic culture that has, over time, been layered beneath the surface in South Tipperary. Explicit in north Clare and less so in Carrick, is collage: culture and its composite elements as formed by disparate and often opposing forces – the Irish and the English languages or traditional music and brass band music, for example – and this is Coady's favoured method of composition in *All Souls*. Finally, nothing represents dispossession as well as traditional music – and the literary music of the dispossessed is at the heart of *All Souls*.

The best explanation of Coady's purpose in *All Souls*, outside of the work itself, is provided in an essay he wrote for the 1995 'Migration and Emigration' issue of *Poetry Ireland Review*. He cites some of the classics of diaspora writing – Brian Friel's *The Loves of Cass Maguire*, Donall Mac Amhlaigh's *Dialan Deoraí*, Micí Mac Gabhann's *Rotha Mór an tSaoil*, Charles Fanning's *The Irish Voice in America*, and the Albany novels of William Kennedy – and provides two commentaries on his interest in the Irish in America, both of which are central to *All Souls*. The first introduces the family narrative:

> In the 1880s my great-grandfather, an impoverished boatman on the Suir, left for America following the death of his wife in childbirth. He left his one surviving child behind in Ireland, effectively abandoning him, only to write a single letter from Philadelphia thirty years later in a plea for understanding and forgiveness. The abandoned child – who became my grandfather – dramatically burned that single letter and never replied.[17]

Such a departure from Carrick-on-Suir and its environs was not unique to the Coady family during the nineteenth century. In his memoir, the singer Liam Clancy, a contemporary of Coady's, describes a similar disruption (though a less secretive one) of Clancy family life during that century. It is a further illustration of the extent to which nineteenth century family life was rendered unstable by poverty, illness, poor health care and emigration:

> Not all of the Clancys, though, could take this subservience. My grandfather's father took off for America, leaving a family of twelve children behind. He settled in Florida and married again. Being a good Catholic, he proceeded to start a family of thirteen children with his new wife. He didn't hide anything, either. One of his descendants, Margaret Clancy of New York, later came back to contribute a new stained glass window to the parish church in Piltown. It's there to this day.[18]

Coady's second commentary is a gloss on Irish emigration itself and the silence that has gathered around it:

> Consider the uncreated conscience of the Irish diaspora. Whatever about cunning, there has certainly been exile and silence. A quite astonishing degree of silence in fact, whether willed or otherwise. Apart from the ballad tradition, the experience of emigration – perhaps the most definitive historical reality for millions of Irish people over the last two centuries – has never articulated itself in anything like a commensurate literature of substance and dimension, either at home or abroad ... Can this extraordinary lacuna in our national discourse, this relative silence relating to one of the central streams of our modern social history and communal

experience, denote some deeply significant hiding-hole of denial and evasive amnesia in the national psyche?[19]

In 'The Use of Memory', the extended final section of *All Souls*, Coady solders the familial and national narratives to indicate the undesirability and impossibility of their separation and sees himself – man and poet – moving fluidly between the two. Coady is the writer who has settled in his hometown but he is also the grandson of his namesake – Michael Coady, the abandoned child – and the son of George Coady who witnessed the arrival of the letter from America and its burning:

> *Silence was the bitter*
> *answer you were given*
> *every empty day*
> *until you died:*
>
> *by a breakfast table*
> *my child father*
> *watched your son unseal*
> *his darkest pain,*
>
> *saw the pages torn and cast*
> *in mortal grief and anger*
> *out of an abandoned child's*
> *unspeakable heart-hunger*
> *into the brute finality*
> *of flame.*[20]

To hear the voices of the past and to recover silent memory from its vast emigrant mass, Coady proceeds to Philadelphia to trace the progress and find the burial place of James Coady, the ancestor who abandoned his child. If he can describe this man's life, he can recover him again for the family, for Carrick and for himself. It is important that the dead and exiled, the doubly dead, become part of the present as this will liberate them and those who have followed them from a lost past and a puzzled future, something that is expressed by T.S. Eliot in lines Coady inserts into 'The Use of Memory', between 'The Letter' and the beginning of his American narrative:

> This is the use of memory:
> For liberation – not less of love but expanding
> Of love beyond desire, and so liberation
> From the future as well as the past.[21]

This long final section is what the book builds towards; however it is worth noting briefly the earlier sections to understand how this work moves towards its superb conclusion. In the first six sections Coady ranges widely. As he has done in his earlier volumes he describes and celebrates aspects of Carrick life, though in *All Souls* he is overwhelmed by the weight these carry across time:

> You begin to feel
> a kind of terror
> at the weight
>
> of what lies stacked
> from floor to ceiling
> all about you.[22]

Coady reaches back into folklore and history to illustrate the extent to which even the battle between St Patrick and Oisín, between the Christian and pre-Christian view, is still relevant to contemporary Ireland. He provides translations of poems written in Irish from the eighteenth century as homages to the final representations of experience in that language at a time when it was fading from South Tipperary forever. Language loss, like emigration, is another mode of dispossession. He forges a collection of sayings heard on the street and in pubs into a section of haiku-like vignettes. In 'The Picture House', he describes the social classes of Carrick and how they are divided:

> Under one roof for fifty years
> our town divided into three;
> balcony, parterre and pit defined
> the truth of caste in our community.[23]

In the title poem, a reverie that takes place as the speaker walks home from the pub, he encounters the living and the dead and records their names, deeds and siphons particulars of their lives, in both Irish and English:

> and there's Mag Delaney at the West Gate
> hearing her own last Act of Contrition
> under the wheels of a Crossley Tender ...[24]

He provides an account of a night in November 1927, when his father and two uncles attended Verdi's *La Forza Del Destino* at the Metropolitan Opera House in New York before his father returned home to live in Carrick. In addition to providing us with a more complex version of the musical tastes of the emigrant Irish than we are accustomed to, this section celebrates the Coady's long family tradition of interest in music and musicianship: opera, brass band music, traditional music. Furthermore allusions are made to jazz, the new sensation of the age, when the narrator interjects, 'in another part of the city on that November evening wasn't the young Duke Ellington raising a storm at The Cotton Club?'[25] Just as Coady's father has returned to Ireland, so too has jazz found a way across the Atlantic to the south east: when his parents-to-be first meet at a dance in the Foresters' Hall 'Duke Ellington's "Solitude" [played] as they danced together'.[26] In common with 'The Blind Arch' and 'The Use of Memory', 'Three Men Standing at the Met' is rendered in prose. The formal effect, therefore, has the feel of musical improvisation.

Writing of James Joyce's *Ulysses*, Karen Lawrence has noted that:

> One can describe *Ulysses* as a book that changes its mind as it progresses and forces a corresponding change of mind in the reader. The segmented quality of *Ulysses* – the discontinuity of the narrative as it dons various stylistic 'masks' – can be treated as successive breaks in 'narrative contracts' and successive rhetorical experiments rather than segments in a spatial whole. The reader of *Ulysses* comes to each chapter

with expectations that are contingent upon what he has experienced not only in other novels but also in the preceding chapters of this one. These expectations are frustrated and altered as the book progresses. The narrative contract we form at the beginning of the book – the implicit agreement between the writer and the reader about the way the book is to be read – is broken.[27]

In *All Souls*, Coady breaks the long-cultivated poetic contract that has developed between Irish poets and readers of their works. At various points the reader must question the very text being read and wonder aloud about what manner of poetry collection this is when it includes as much prose as poetry and contains photographs, parts of an opera programme, elements of a family tree, in addition to the familiar lyrics and translations which, when mixed-in with the unusual elements, are rendered strange. Like *Ulysses*, *All Souls* is full of discontinuities – of time, place and multiple genres – which give it its formal originality. Also particular sections of *Ulysses* and *All Souls* have much in common: Joyce's Circe chapter and Coady's 'All Souls' are both mad, rhapsodic rambles through the city/town at night. Like *Ulysses*, *All Souls* is a modernist text though one written sixty years later. It has much in common, too, with Eliot's *The Waste Land* and Pound's *Cantos* in its use of collage, its poet/reader contract breaking and its multilingualism. Although multilingualism is usually associated with colonialism and postcolonialism in Irish critical discourse, Coady reminds us that it is also a product of modernism. Joyce, as Karen Lawrence points out, retains a basic fidelity to fact with the result that *Ulysses* is always grounded in realism and the same can be said of *All Souls*.

Coady's debt to Joyce is further confirmation of the influence that Joyce has had on Irish poets, as Dillon Johnston has explained. In addition to these more obvious literary influences, I would hazard that two modes of musical expression have played parts in framing the poetic structure of *All Souls*: traditional music and jazz. From traditional music heard in Doolin and elsewhere Coady noted how the individual musician simultaneously repeats and alters the jig or reel being played, while from jazz he learned an even more radical mode of experimentation and collage. For Alfred Appel Jr, in *Jazz Modernism: From Ellington and Armstrong to Matisse and Joyce*, modernist literature, painting, sculpture and jazz are wrought, to a large degree, from the same hard ground, share similar artistic ploys; all of this has filtered down to Coady who, as already noted, informs us that his parents first danced to Ellington's 'Solitude'. In the United States, from the Black Mountain and Beat poets to the present, jazz is often cited as an important influence on how poetry is composed. Of modern Irish poetry collections, Ciaran Carson's *Belfast Confetti* comes closest to *All Souls* as it too is a compendium of various poetic forms and literary genres; Carson is also a musician and poet. What Carson has written of Dante's youth can also be applied to Joyce, Carson and Coady:

> 'In his youth,' says Boccaccio, 'Dante took the greatest delight in music and song; and with all the best singers and musicians of those times he was in friendship and familiarity.'[28]

From a purely visual aspect, John Montague's *The Rough Field* has much in common with *All Souls*: in both works the visual images are important narrative, poetic and rhetorical devices. In his reading of *All Souls*, Daniel Tobin privileges the poem's visual elements by noting its 'bricolage structure, its organisation around bits and pieces' and how the poem, like a movie, is delivered, then undermined, by 'voices and voiceovers'.[29] Both readings point to the modernist path that Coady has chosen to walk. A final twist in the issue of genre is provided by the dramatic elements present in *All Souls*: in 1997 Coady's arrangement for multiple voices of the poem 'All Souls' was given public readings in Kilkenny, Waterford and at the book's launch in Carrick and 'Three Men Standing at the Met' was broadcast on RTÉ Radio 1 in 2001.[30]

At the heart of 'The Use of Memory' is Coady's question: 'Can words upon the page restore a lost and broken man to the fractured hearthstone of kinship?'[31] Coady relates the story of Michael, the abandoned child, who rose from poverty to middle-class respectability in Carrick while, at the same time, remaining tortured and wounded by his father's desertion of him, as he so dramatically proclaimed by tearing up the letter in which his father sought forgiveness and reconciliation. The author also searches for James, the father who abandoned his son and unearths a fable of poverty, sadness, ill-health and alcoholism played out in New York and Philadelphia and ending with his death in 1915:

> Ireland is often ignorant of the realities of Irish immigrant life in America. We have heard of the trumpeted successes, some of mythically rare proportions, while below those spectacular pinnacles we may be able to guess at an extensive grey middle ground of survival and modest achievement over generations. What remains largely unrecorded is the limbo world of those who sank in failure, the type of wasteland of social disconnection, drift and dereliction memorably recreated and redeemed by William Kennedy in his 'Albany' trilogy and notably *Ironweed*.[32]

While in Philadelphia, James Coady married for a second time and Mary, like his first wife, also died while giving birth – to a stillborn girl. Another daughter died in infancy and neither of his sons lived beyond their second decade. Michael Coady objectively records the information he has gathered in America while positioning himself outside of the moral debate. At the same time he restores the narrative of James Coady's life to the larger narratives of family, town and nation, so that he is recovered from the silence of the past just as John Montague's emigrant family is recovered from Brooklyn in *The Dead Kingdom*. For the reader the crime committed by James Coady is lessened when seen in the context of the hard life he encountered in America and by the fact that his son was probably better cared for by his grandfather in Carrick than he could have been by his desperate father in America.

Although *All Souls* calls on Irish readers and writers to pay greater attention to the diaspora, it is primarily a vehicle for Coady's personal voyage to bond with what he refers to as *'presequence'*, or 'a knowing return to a seminal moment in the past from its own future'.[33] He arrives in Philadelphia to walk in James Coady's footsteps, to find his grave and learn the ironic news that of James Coady's offspring the only child to enjoy a long life was the abandoned child in Ireland. In Philadelphia, Coady is brought deep into the Irish history of the city. He attends Mass at St Philip de Neri church where James and Mary Coady worshipped, where their children were baptised and where their requiem masses were offered in 1893 and 1915, respectively. He recalls the anti-Irish-Catholic riots of 1844 which necessitated the deployment of 5000 troops on the streets of the city and a memorial sermon preached in Irish at St Philip's in 1847 to mark the death of Daniel O'Connell. Coady notes that the streets where the Coadys lived are clustered together and near the river and is reminded of Carrick:

> All of the successive addresses I find are in an area as compact as that between Carrick's Main Street and the river Suir, with the same pattern of street cluster fronted by a river, the configuration differing only in scale.[34]

His research, reading and walking allows Michael Coady a glimpse of James Coady's hopeless American Dream. Also the mystery at the centre of the family's narrative is revealed and described so that anger and loss are converted into understanding and empathy. To underscore this new reality Coady introduces two powerful notes of epiphany. The first occurs in the church in Philadelphia:

> Nothing prepares my already heightened imagination for what dramatically explodes out of the blue during the Mass – the church suddenly darkening, wind through the wide open

> windows whirling and scattering prayer leaflets, the cosmic flare and crackle of lightning, the shattering detonation of thunder and cloudburst even as the priest raises the chalice. In my suggestible state I am shaken by it, as by some kind of dramatic Pentecostal visitation ...[35]

The heavens have opened and the Gods have spoken to honour James Coady's rescue from silence and to celebrate the completion of Michael Coady's journey. It is a gesture of continuance, not closure. The second epiphany appears at the end of *All Souls* with the news that Michael and Martina Coady's third child has been named Michael James:

> The summer of 1990 brought the birth of our third child, a son. We named the infant Michael James for reconciliation and Marcus for remembrance of his mother's father. From the later migration by another James, a Coady in Connecticut made his christening shawl. The basket weaver made his crib.[36]

Even though 'The Use of Memory' is written in prose, the closing pages, because of the presence of rich epiphanies, are statements of faith in the moment and in the power of the lyrical impulse and the lyric poem. In this way it is linked to Coady's earliest poems. Fittingly enough, for a work that pushes the borders of Irish poetry, the last word is spoken by a photograph: it's of the Suir, its bridge and weir and of a man and child posing for the camera near Oven Lane. *One Another*, the 2003 volume that follows *All Souls*, makes use of similar methods of composition and orchestration to explore further aspects of Carrick-on-Suir's various histories. It is worth noting that Coady is one of a very small group of rural-born Irish writers who have lived almost all of their adult lives in the places where they were born and reared. In 1998, he was elected to Aosdána, the academy of Irish writers and artists.

In 'A Local Habitation', a talk aired on RTÉ1 in 2000, Coady took time to take measure of his life as a writer:

> So unlike most writers, I still live where I was born. I've remained on site and that compels and enables an intimate

> focus: the vertical as well as the horizontal dimension of space. The horizontal is what you see: the people currently walking around, the state of the tide at this moment on the river, who is being buried or born today. The vertical dimension is the absent presence, what lies underneath and invisibly all around; the deep, deep accumulation of lives and living on the site ...[37]

Although he returned after college to his hometown to live, it was, as he has pointed out, the luck of a teaching position becoming available as soon as he had qualified, and family circumstances that made his return possible. Over the last decade and a half, Michael Coady has produced important work both as poet and essayist that has culminated in *All Souls*, a work of daring originality and fierce passion that recovers from history those silenced, often broken, voices of the diaspora. Thinking of Micho Russell, Coady wonders 'what is a living tradition but the people who carry and embody it, individually and communally'.[38] Certainly, Coady himself embodies all that is important in the poetry of Ireland.

NOTES

1. Ciaran Carson, 'The Basket Weaver's Hands', *Poetry Ireland Review*, 58, Autumn 1998, pp 30–31.
2. Theo Dorgan, '*All Souls*', *Newsletter of the Munster Literature Centre*. Summer 1998, p. 3.
3. Caitriona O'Reilly, 'Ding-an-Sich', *The Irish Times*, 21 February 1998, p. 6.
4. 'Two for a Woman, Three for a Man', *Two for a Woman, Three for a Man* (Gallery Press, 1980), p. 20.
5. 'Still Life from a Hill over a Town', *Ibid*, p. 23.
6. *Ibid*.
7. *Ibid*, p. 20.
8. 'Eavan Boland, A Habitable Grief', *The Lost Land* (Norton, 1998), p. 29.
9. *Full Tide* (Relay Books, 1999), p. 67.
10. Daniel Tobin, 'The Parish and Lost America: Michael Coady's *All Souls* (1997)', *New Hibernia Review*, 7:3, Autumn, 2003, p. 42.
11. 'Letting Go', *Oven Lane* (Gallery Press, 1987), p. 11.
12. 'The Letter', *Ibid*, p. 27.

13 'The Pursuit of Happiness', *Ibid*, p. 63.
14 'Stopping by a Clare Graveyard After Hours', *Ibid*, p. 37.
15 *Ibid*.
16 *The Well of Spring Water: A Memoir of Pakie and Micho Russell of Doolin, County Clare* (Carrick-on-Suir, Co. Tipperary, 1996, n.p.), p. 11.
17 'The Sea-Divided Silence', *Poetry Ireland Review*, 46, Summer 1995, p. 34.
18 Liam Clancy, *The Mountain of the Women: Memoirs of an Irish Troubadour* (Doubleday, 2002), p. 14.
19 'The Sea-Divided Silence', p. 28.
20 'The Use of Memory', *All Souls*, p. 84.
21 *Ibid*, p. 85.
22 'The Public Record', *All Souls*, p. 26.
23 'The Picture House', *All Souls*, p. 31.
24 'All Souls', *All Souls*, p. 50.
25 'Three Men Standing at the Met', *All Souls*, p. 41.
26 *Ibid*, p. 44.
27 Karen Lawrence, *The Odyssey of Style in Ulysses* (Princeton University Press, 1981), p. 6.
28 Ciaran Carson, *The Inferno of Dante Alighieri* (Granta Publications, 2002), p. xxi.
29 Tobin, p. 37.
30 'Acknowledgements', *All Souls*, p. 138.
31 'The Use of Memory', *All Souls*, p. 108.
32 *Ibid*.
33 *Ibid*, p. 88.
34 *Ibid*, p. 121.
35 *Ibid*, p. 118.
36 *Ibid*, p. 135.
37 'A Local Habitation', John Quinn, producer, RTÉ Radio 1, 12 July 2000, p. 2.
38 *Ibid*, p. 4.

REFERENCES

Appel. Jr., Alfred, *Jazz Modernism: From Ellington and Armstrong to Matisse and Joyce* (Knopf, 2000).

Boland, Eavan, *Object Lessons: The Life of a Woman and the Poet in Our Time* (Norton, 1995).

Carson, Ciaran, *Belfast Confetti* (Gallery Press, 1989).

Coady, Michael, *All Souls* (Gallery Press, 1997, revised edition 2001).

Given Light (Gallery Press, 2017)
Going by Water (Gallery Press, 2009).
One Another (Gallery Press, 2003).
Oven Lane (Gallery Press, 1987).
'Three Men Standing at the Met', John Quinn, producer, RTÉ Radio 1, 23 December 2001.
Fanning, Charles, *The Irish Voice in America* (University of Kentucky Press, 1990).
Friel, Brian, *The Loves of Cass Maguire* (Faber, 1967).
Johnston, Dillon, *Irish Poetry after Joyce* (Syracuse University Press, 1998).
Joyce, James, *Ulysses* (Vintage, 1986).
Kennedy, William, *Ironweed* (Viking, 1983).
Mac Amhlaigh, Donall, *Dialann Deoraí* (An Clóchomhar, 1960).
Mac Gabhann, Micí, *Rotha Mór an tSaoil* (Foilseacháin Náisiúnta Teoranta, 1959).
Mahon, Derek, *Collected Poems* (Gallery Press, 1999).
Montague, John, *The Dead Kingdom* (Wake Forest University Press, 1984).
The Rough Field (Wake Forest University Press, 1989, 5th edition).

From Abiquiu to Cerrillos:
In Search of Georgia O'Keeffe

On this day last year I stood with a group waiting to be taken across the road from the parking lot adjacent to the Abiquiu Inn to Georgia O'Keeffe's Abiquiu home. Behind me meandered the main road to Santa Fe that O'Keeffe had observed from her studio and obsessively photographed and painted and the cottonwood trees that lent shape and definition to these works:

> Two walls of my room in the Abiquiu house are glass and from one window I see the road toward Española, Santa Fe and the world. The road fascinates me with its ups and downs and finally its wide sweep as it speeds toward the wall of my hilltop to go past me.[1]

An admirer of her work, I had come to New Mexico to observe but also to trace, if this were possible, the Irish American aspect of her work. My inquiries were the result of a decade's interest in O'Keeffe's paintings, with my research guided by studies of her work, biographies and autobiographies and visits to museums as well as books written by literary scholars – Charles Fanning's *The Irish*

Voice in America and Daniel Tobin's *Awake in America: On Irish American Poetry* in particular.

I wondered if O'Keeffe was more Irish American in name than in practice following Fanning's belief, or whether front-loaded material mattered, an idea that embraces Tobin's view that identities even if denied by artists – 'doubleness' is a term he is fond of – are always operating in the background, a reprise perhaps of Harold Bloom's anxiety of influence trope.[2] Both Fanning and Tobin are master scholars with each offering cogent arguments and I like to think that I can see both sides evenly. Also in the back of my mind was Rebecca Solnit's belief that we live in many spaces simultaneously – an idea that held emotional weight for me.[3] Of course, Georgia O'Keeffe's personal and artistic odyssey, as Roxana Robinson recounts it, was so many-sided that it appears resistant to narrow categorisation. It is likely that O'Keeffe, a modernist more than anything else, worked as an artist without hyphens: like Joyce, she is local and international, rather than ethnic or even national. I wondered if clues to O'Keeffe's Irish voice could be found at Abiquiu, Ghost Ranch and in the landscapes of northern New Mexico. It was this curiosity that had brought me here. Our bus arrived. We climbed onboard.

The Abiquiu house had been owned by the local Catholic archdiocese and, after years of dreaming that she might someday own it, O'Keeffe, in December 1945, was finally able to purchase the property for $500 down and a tax-deductible gift of $2500. In 1949, with the house completely finished to her specifications:

> she moved from New York to make New Mexico her permanent home ... She usually lived in the Abiquiu house winter and fall and at the Ghost Ranch house spring and summer, but she made frequent trips between both houses throughout the year.[4]

The house is a pueblo revival-style hacienda. O'Keeffe described her house and the impulse to buy it as follows:

> My house in Abiquiu is pretty empty; only what I need is in it. I like empty walls. I've only left up two Arthur Dove's, some African sculpture and a little of my own stuff. I bought the place because it had that door in the patio, the one I have painted so often. I had no peace till I bought the house.[5]

Though she remained connected to New York and the wider world through the distribution of her work, effectively she had cut her ties with the city. Now, New Mexico was home and the place that centred her.

The O'Keeffe family, recently emigrated from Co. Cork, arrived in Sun Prairie, Wisconsin, in 1848. Pierce O'Keeffe and his wife Catherine Mary Shorthall, Georgia O'Keeffe's Irish grandparents, had travelled by ship from Liverpool to New York where they had disembarked on 22 April, continuing their trip overland and on the Great Lakes to Milwaukee; from there, they had proceeded by oxcart to Sun Prairie to farm land they had bought from the government.[6] As Roxana Robinson points out, they brought 'portable elements of their lives in Ireland – emblematic elements: family silver and a china tea service', an indication that even though they left Ireland in the wake of the Great Famine, they did so with valuables intact. In Cork, the O'Keeffe's wool business was affected by high taxes and this was a spur to emigrate. O'Keeffe's maternal grandparents, the Tottos, were Hungarian, her grandfather a count who had been exiled for 'his participation in the 1848 Revolution of Hungary against Austria'.[7] Indirectly and directly, both the O'Keeffes and Tottos were victims of events and alignments in their home countries that pushed them to seek new beginnings in America. As families caught in political strife and economic upheaval the O'Keeffes and Tottos were typical American immigrants – both then and now. Ida Totto, their daughter, was twenty when Frank O'Keeffe, then thirty-one, proposed to her in 1884. It was noted that Frank had 'strikingly Celtic good looks'.[8] The O'Keeffes and Tottos occupied adjoining farms with the O'Keeffes eventually acquiring the Tottos' holding after the count returned to Hungary, abandoning his family in Wisconsin. The Tottos were Lutheran, the O'Keeffes Catholic: Frank and Ida were married in an Episcopal Church and disagreed on religious matters over a lifetime.

Georgia Totto O'Keeffe, the second of seven children, was born on 15 November 1887. Later on, O'Keeffe asserted that she was more like her Irish father than Hungarian mother, 'I think that deep down I am like my father. When he wanted to see the country, he just got up and went'.[9] While a student at the Art Students' League in New York, her looks were commented on by her peers:

> the young men at the League found the twenty-year-old Georgia very appealing. Her surname and her curly hair revealed her Irish blood, and she was given the feminine form of the nickname awarded the ubiquitous immigrant: 'Patsy'.[10]

Though the nickname was likely conferred without malice, one bristles at it because it confers on the young artist recently arrived from the Midwest an aura of the other, rather than of the aspiring painter. Perhaps it was a great novelty for her fellow students to behold an Irish American artist at a time when they were more used to thinking of such women as individuals who helped middle and upper-class women run their households.

Georgia O'Keeffe expressed great fondness for Sun Prairie:

> I remembered the beautiful fields of grain and wheat out there – like snow – only yellow ... in spring ... They were plowing and there were patterns of plowed ground and patches where things were growing.[11]

Similarly, the simple built environment caught her attention, 'The barn is a very healthy part of me', she wrote years later. 'It is something that I know ... it is my childhood'.[12] Throughout her life, like the Irish poet Richard Murphy, built environments would help frame her artistic endeavours. Her childhood Wisconsin landscape was both home and teacher and what she absorbed from it prepared her for others that would be defining of her adult life as an artist: in New York City, Lake George, northern New Mexico and their natural and built environments. The lore of place, living in a mental, moral and artistic space that allowed for free communion between person and place were matters that absorbed O'Keeffe throughout her lifetime. Place has long been both an Irish obsession and burden – and O'Keeffe was absorbed by it, in multiples. This attachment to Wisconsin is quite similar to her contemporary Willa Cather's attachment to the area surrounding Red Cloud, Nebraska. Like Cather and Joyce, O'Keeffe has been able to understand place objectively so as not to be confined by it and to move between different places with the result that she, like Cather, can subtly reinvent herself as an artist when the locus shifts elsewhere. In *Song of the Lark*, Thea Kronborg, the young singer, is drawn into the landscape of northern Arizona in a fashion and at a depth that parallels the intensity of O'Keeffe's engagement with New Mexico:

> She was getting back to the earliest sources of gladness that she could remember. She had loved the sun, and the brilliant solitudes of sand and sun, long before these other things had come along to fasten themselves upon her and torment her. That night, when she clambered into her big German feather bed, she felt completely released from the enslaving desire to get on in the world. Darkness had once again the sweet wonder that it had in childhood.[13]

Though both O'Keeffe and Cather engaged deeply with the Southwest, New Mexico and Arizona, respectively, these served primarily as locations that drew both women toward new work which opened up new pathways, or re-opened old pathways that had been closed off. Here both women could unlearn and grow. Cather's Thea Kronborg is in flight from her voice teacher in Chicago while O'Keeffe is in revolt against her teachers:

> It was in the fall of 1915 that I first had the idea that what I had been taught was of little value to me except for the use of my materials as a language.[14]

New Mexico allowed O'Keeffe to explore and trust her own true nature and keen instincts as she explains in her autobiography:

> I have always picked flowers where I found them – have picked up sea shells and rocks and pieces of wood where there were sea shells and rocks and pieces of wood that I liked ... When I found the beautiful white bones on the desert I picked them up and took them home too ... I have used these things to say what is to me the wideness and wonder of the world as I live in it.[15]

It is worth noting that these two great American cultural figures were exploring the Southwest contemporaneously. In the literary world we are pushed to accept the journeys made by Hemingway and Fitzgerald to France and Spain as defining moments in American cultural development and to zealously guard these as versions of cultural truth. In my view other journeys are more alive and resulted in superior work: O'Keeffe's to New Mexico and Cather's to Arizona. Joyce, of course, rarely shifts his focal point from Dublin though his style changes between and within novels, while Cather, somewhat more traditional in her formal structures, embraced wide thematic and locational challenges. O'Keeffe is a true original and inimitable, like Joyce.

As I entered Georgia O'Keeffe's Abiquiu property I was reminded of a story my father was fond of recounting. He liked to recall a cartoon he had once seen in *Dublin Opinion*. One figure announced that Yuri Gagarin had become the first man to ascend into space. His companion wondered how much time would elapse before the *Irish Independent* established Gagarin's Irish connection or *bona fide*. With this warning in the back of my mind, I harboured the uncomfortable thought that I had come to Abiquiu to fraudulently anoint O'Keeffe as an Irish American to suit a narrative my own father had warned me against making. For an hour or more, our group was led through O'Keeffe's home and garden. What a rare privilege it was to walk through her kitchen – most of the white cabinets and appliances purchased from the Sears catalogue – to observe from a short distance her living room with the modernist, uncomfortable Eileen Grayish furniture. Then her studio and bedroom. I saw doors and windows I had seen in paintings. I looked at landscapes that O'Keeffe had seen each day. Often the thought occurred to me that I was standing behind the artist as she painted, that eventually she would turn around to seek my opinion. Defensively I would raise my hands and smile. It was such a privilege to be here.

The stark simplicity of her bedroom brought to mind a monastic cell; however, this could not be judged with any conviction as a gesture towards her Irish Catholic heritage because she was equally interested in Japanese style and in twentieth century minimalism, both of which the semiotics of her bedroom exposed to our view. The severity of the room was an expression of style but also an aspect of an overriding structure as Robinson explains, 'O'Keeffe held that art is, itself, a moral structure, and that by adhering to its principles the artist upholds those of a universal moral system'.[16] As she revived and remodelled this building that would become her home, O'Keeffe followed Vasily Kandinsky, one of her important influences, who believed that 'the artist must have something to say for mastery over form is not his goal but rather adapting of form to its inner meaning'.[17] She did not seek to impose a hard-edged ideology on the building she was remodelling; instead, she sought to follow the form that the building had gifted her, and this same view would guide her representation of the landscape of New Mexico. A traditional Irish American attitude could not foreground such an undertaking, for many reasons. First, it would be impossible to get any group of people to agree on any one definition of such an attitude. Second, Georgia O'Keeffe's background and religious upbringing was not traditionally Irish American, and, above all else, she was always an individual resistant to labelling. To have followed an Irish American path would have been restrictive: Irish America was but a layer of her being that only partially and obliquely defined her.

O'Keeffe shaped her home to reflect her wide moral/aesthetic viewpoints and this was evident throughout. The free interplay of the ancient and the modern was exciting to absorb, though it made it impossible to trace its provenance with any degree of certainty. Abiquiu was not Irish American in the way that the interior of a New York apartment in an Alice McDermott's novel is, for example. Homes in such novels as *At Weddings and Wakes* are muted, conservative, neo-Victorian monochrome in stark contrast to O'Keeffe's fondness for light, air, colour and ideas of space founded on a minimalist aesthetic. Simultaneously, Abiquiu's parts contributed to and took away from its whole. While walking through a room, one sensed the larger impact of its design; then, stopping to observe an item of furniture, one became absorbed in it to the exclusion of the other objects it belonged to. Most of all, Abiquiu revealed to me aspects of the individuality of its owner who articulated her sentiments as the home was being remodelled, 'and inch by inch it is becoming – my house – something that feels like my shell to live in'.[18] Abiquiu would be both a secure haven, a point of departure and return and also, like the snail shell, inseparable from the artist's body. Perhaps, at some deep level and across generations, some immigrants harbour dreams of return, of undertaking journeys homeward to places of origin, as Wallace Stevens has articulated so well:

> Who is my father in this world, in this house,
> At the spirit's base?
>
> My father's father, his father's father, his –
> Shadows like winds
>
> Go back to a parent before thought, before speech,
> At the head of the past[19]

Stevens' 'head of the past' is a remote point on the west of Ireland in a country that he never visited. For others such a place may emerge from a genealogical fable. For O'Keeffe it was an old property that she made her own.

If we can accept that trauma can be passed down through generations, we might also imagine that a desire to return to a more mythic home could drive peoples' dreams and psyches. In *At Weddings and Wakes*, Alice McDermott shows that this dynamic can also operate in another way with the Irish American family, now split between the city and the suburbs, viewing the old apartment in Brooklyn as the family's ancestral space rather than an imagined location in Ireland. O'Keeffe, I suspect, found a similar sense of security and belonging in Abiquiu. McDermott's Irish Americans founded their own Ireland in Brooklyn; O'Keeffe's country was more independent of influence as she would not allow herself to be narrowed by strictures. To make that journey back to one's place of origin is equally attractive and impossible. Today the old Irish homestead is the property of strangers who might not extend the hand of welcome, while the mother's womb, the deepest of all places of origin, has for a long time been an unfeasible option. One must look elsewhere. For Stevens, the place of origin was a place in Ireland he had never visited – a supreme fiction; for McDermott's family in *At Weddings and Wakes* it was a simple Brooklyn apartment; and for Georgia O'Keeffe it was this home in New Mexico through which I walked.

O'Keeffe had first come to New Mexico in 1917 while on vacation with her youngest sister Claudia:

On both ends of the roundabout trip, the two sisters stopped off in Santa Fe, New Mexico. The pale, clean quiet adobe town, the pure glittering air, and the exhilaration of the high mesa country made the encounter one of great resonance for Georgia. She wrote to Stieglitz that the trip had 'virtually washed the slate clean of Canyon – NY – the past.' For O'Keeffe, the 1917 encounter was brief. But the land of New Mexico remained – as had the white bones on the high desert and the cries of the penned cattle – deeply settled within her mind. 'From then on,' she said later, 'I was always on my way back'.[20]

I left Abiquiu. It was late afternoon and the light had begun to fade. The next day walking in O'Keeffe's footsteps through Ghost Ranch and along dry river beds where she had tramped, I thought about this phrase ('I was always on my way back') and wondered if my presence here, my pursuit of O'Keeffe, was nothing larger than an expression of my own desire to return to New Mexico. Twenty years before I had come here for the first time and been so overwhelmed and puzzled by its singular beauty that, since then, I have availed of every opportunity to come back. If none were available I invented one. To think of New Mexico warms my heart, though to offer some contrast I should note that an Albuquerque taxi driver informed me once that I would not think of New Mexico in such glowing terms if I lived here full-time! On another level, I wondered if, as an immigrant, I had sublimated one homeland for another. If home was far away, it was New Mexico not Ireland. Leaving Abiquiu that day and thinking back on it later that evening, I was careful not to make claims that could not be substantiated, I was aware that much research needed to be done. O'Keeffe's library at Abiquiu was off-limits so I wondered what story might her collection tell and had a catalogue of her books been compiled? At another level the visit had reminded me it is not ethnic origin that matters most of all: the woman or man in the studio is first and foremost the artist engaged in some activity that is singular. What Willa Cather writes of Thea Kronborg is equally true of Georgia O'Keeffe:

> Artistic growth is, more than it is anything else, a refining of the sense of truthfulness ... That afternoon nothing new came to Thea Kronborg, no enlightenment, no inspiration. She merely came into full possession of things she had been refining and perfecting for so long. Her inhibitions chanced to be fewer than usual, and, within herself, she entered into an inheritance that she herself had laid up, into the fullness of the faith she had kept before she knew its name or its meaning.[21]

To have had the opportunity to have visited the home and surrounding areas where O'Keeffe had touched her fullest and deepest 'inheritance' was a privilege and deeply moving – at a level beyond such ordinary matters as genealogy and research.

My companion on the trip was my wife Drucilla, herself both a writer and scholar. The daughter of an art history teacher father and an artist mother, she had had her fill of both subjects by the onset of her teenage years. Of course, she has a deep understanding of the lore and legend of the American southwest and was therefore happy to accompany me to visit places that she had read about but had not as yet had an opportunity to visit. As long as the fine art appreciation part of the trip was kept within reasonable limits she would remain amenable. Her real interest on this trip was turquoise: she hoped to learn more about it and, negotiations with vendors going well, acquire some. Leaving Abiquiu, we drove to Santa Fe where she spent an afternoon browsing among the shops and haggling with vendors on the plaza. The next morning, in keeping with the turquoise theme, we took the old road from Santa Fe to Albuquerque, called the Turquoise Trail. Hitting the road I felt that my period of professional inquiry in New Mexico had concluded: I looked forward to a wide-open, relaxing Sunday.

While walking though the ramshackle museum in Cerrillos, a small, old down-at-the heel town along the Turquoise Trail, I came across the figure of James P. McNulty, described as a legendary figure in New Mexico: an Irish American who had come to New Mexico to seek his fortune. Quickly, I regained my scholarly pose: taking notes and pledging to follow up at a later time. The light was not good in the museum, an edifice that brought back to me the description of the ramshackle, add-on family home in Anne Enright's *The Gathering* – described as being more extension than home. The museum's official title is the Casa Grande Trading Post, Cerrillos Mining Museum and Petting Zoo. When one tired of the items on display in the gift shop and museum, one could join family groups wandering through the Petting Zoo. In truth, the zoo's simplicity and singular sense of purpose was a relief from the museum's visual onslaught and sensory overload.

In a document he filed as he sought an increase in his military pension, McNulty provided some interesting details related to his life and service. He was born in County Sligo on 16 March 1846 or 1847, immigrating to America and joining the US Army in 1866 in New York. He fought in both the Civil War and the Indian Wars, served under Custer among others and was discharged from the Army at Camp Trinidad, Colorado, in May 1889. From around 1880 till his death in 1933, McNulty lived in Cerrillos. In a long obituary published in the *New Mexican* on 26 January 1933, McNulty's birthplace is erroneously cited as Central City, Colorado; after his discharge from the army he had worked as a miner there before coming to New Mexico to manage the Turquoise Mines for the Tiffany Company of New York, at that time considered the best-producing turquoise mine in the United States. Eventually, when the value of turquoise dropped, McNulty acquired the mine from the Tiffany Company.

For the most part, McNulty was poorly treated by the Tiffany Company: they were slow to pay his wages with the result that he was often six months in arrears and he found it hard to keep his mining staff from quitting when wages were paid so irregularly. Throughout his time in Cerrillos, Tiffany's mining claim was contested by local landowners, both long-standing and newly arrived and by Native American tribes, and McNulty was cast in the uncomfortable position of representing the Tiffany Company who were easterners and somewhat despised. From someone from rural Ireland, McNulty's plight and position was in equal portions familiar, dangerous and ironic. As a refugee from famine Ireland, McNulty was one of many dispossessed of home, family and country who had come to America in the hopes of finding some measure of prosperity. Working for the Tiffany Company in Cerrillos he had now become an agent of dispossession himself as he worked to keep Native Americans away from the resources and lands they considered their own. Here McNulty was also the agent for an absentee landlord; in truth, I suppose, he was everything that he could not and would not have been in his native Ireland. In his case the need to survive required equal measures of reinvention and amnesia.

The *New Mexican* obituary provides a bizarre account of the settling of one of McNulty's many disputes with Native Americans:

> The taking over of these mines by the Tiffany firm led to intermittent troubles with the Santo Domingo Indians and more than once McNulty, as custodian of the mines, had groups of these Indians hauled into the state courts to prosecute them for trespassing. McNulty charged that Indians were taking out the turquoise for their jewelry work, and that they sent bands of turquoise hunters to the mines to work in the moonlight. It was the late George Volney Howard, lawyer of Santa Fe and later El Paso, also a picturesque character, who defended the Indians in one of his matchless addresses to the

jury, in which he referred to the Indians as the 'poor horny-handed sons of toil.' The Indians got off.[22]

Life at that time was both dangerous and complex. In part, McNulty was able to survive and prosper by engagement in communities; of particular importance is his organising of a Masonic Lodge in Cerrillos with his original mining partner Mike O'Neill, a step that established him among like-minded businessmen throughout the state. In New Mexico the Irish were automatically considered Anglos. It is as a result of research carried out by Patricia McGraw, McNulty's great-grand-daughter, that we now have learned so much about his life in New Mexico. For my part, coming to New Mexico in search of Georgia O'Keeffe and being left with a puzzle rather than a result – though this is nothing to complain about – I rejoiced in finding McNulty, whom I had not heard about and stumbled upon accidently. Serendipity renews one's faith in research. Instead of meeting dead ends, new possibilities can emerge. While my wife explored the endless boxes of stones flung about on trestles, I sat outside in late autumn sunshine enchanted by the complexities of attachment for O'Keeffe, McNulty and myself. I had not fallen into the trap of claiming false belongings to Irish narratives that my father had warned me about. In fact, what I had absorbed on this trip to New Mexico made me want to place all three of us at a greater distance from Ireland than I might have thought possible beforehand. America allows for re-invention. At the same time, like lint, the past attaches itself to the immigrant's garments.

In *A Book of Migrations*, her recounting of her journey through Ireland and her engagement with its urban and rural spaces, Rebecca Solnit casts her being in Ireland in this light:

> In a sense, it was travel itself that I was after. There's a convenient fiction preserved in travel literature, if nowhere else, that a person is wholly in one place at one time ... We are

> often in two places at once. In fact, we are usually in at least two places, and occasionally the contrast is evident ... The new and unknown places called forth strange, oft-forgotten correspondences and desires in the mind, so that the motion of travel takes place as much in the psyche as anywhere else. Travel offers the opportunity to find out who else one is, in that collapse of identity into geography I want to trace.[23]

Though my journey to Abiquiu had failed to yield an Irish American Georgia O'Keeffe, or at best had resulted in an Irish-American-toned O'Keeffe, it was hardly a failure. In addition to stumbling upon James Patrick McNulty, I had been able to trace what Solnit so elegantly describes as 'the collapse of identity into geography'. As an artist, O'Keeffe had collapsed her own identity in the spaces around Abiquiu and Ghost Ranch with monumental results. Through her work, we encounter aspects germane to New Mexico's core.

McNulty's collapse into the geography was of a more practical nature – working the turquoise mine in the belly of the earth – to provide raw materials for exquisite craftwork. Both depended on the financial might of New York dealers: O'Keeffe fared well thanks to Alfred Stieglitz and others while McNulty, on the other hand, was strung along and mistreated by the Tiffany Corporation. Though McNulty's work was quite different from O'Keeffe's, they shared an utter absorption in their chosen areas of New Mexico. Both died in Santa Fe. They represent generational strands of the Irish diaspora, a phenomenon that is more complex and interesting than some might credit: McNulty making multiple stops on his journey from famine-ravaged Ireland to Cerrillos and O'Keeffe, born in part into an Irish American home, folding her identity into modernism, the light of heritage just barely traceable in her life and work. Just as Solnit's Irishness is an accidental blessing, the result of detective work by a relative who dug-up unknown relatives that entitled her to an Irish passport, so too is my own attraction to and experience of being in New Mexico accidental. It is a space I see through eyes trained in Co. Wexford. I too have collapsed my own identity into geography – New Mexico in this instance. O'Keeffe saw Sun Prairie in Abiquiu. We do not know if McNulty saw Carrowmore and Knocknarea in the land that surrounded his turquoise mine.

In his history of the O'Keeffe clan, Gerald O'Keeffe notes that Georgia 'was unquestionably ... proud of her Irishness and had as is described by her great-nephew and great-niece a wonderfully wicked sense of Irish humour'.[24] In addition to providing some updated information on her roots and family in County Cork, Gerald O'Keeffe also highlights an honour bestowed on this great American artist in Ireland – the visual arts space at St Brendan's School in Rathcoole, Mallow, County Cork, is named the *Georgia O'Keeffe Visual Arts Room at St Brendan's School*.

NOTES

1. Georgia O'Keeffe, *Georgia O'Keeffe* (Penguin, 1977), p. 104.
2. Daniel Tobin, *Awake in America: On Irish American Poetry* (University of Notre Dame Press, 2011), p. ix.
3. Rebecca Solnit, *A Book of Migrations* (Verso, 2011, revised ed. orig. 1997), pp 9–10.
4. Barbara Buhler Lynes and Agapita Judy Lopez, *Georgia O'Keeffe and Her Houses: Ghost Ranch and Abiquiu* (Abrams in association with Georgia O'Keeffe Museum, 2012), p. 112.
5. *Ibid*, p. 169.
6. Roxana Robinson, *Georgia O'Keeffe: A Life* (Harper & Row, 1989), p. 6.
7. *Ibid*, p. 6.
8. *Ibid*, p. 4.
9. *Ibid*, p. 22.
10. *Ibid*, pp 57–59.
11. *Ibid*, p. 3.
12. *Ibid*, p. 19.
13. Willa Cather, *The Song of the Lark* (Vintage Classics, 1999), p. 272.
14. *Georgia O'Keeffe*, p. 1.
15. *Ibid*, p. 71.

16   Robinson, p. 352.
17   *Ibid*, p. 108.
18   Lynes and Lopez, p. 223.
19   Wallace Stevens, 'The Irish Cliffs of Moher' in Daniel Tobin (ed.), *The Book of Irish American Poetry: From the Eighteenth Century to the Present* (University of Notre Dame Press, 2007), p. 89.
20   Robinson, pp 189–90.
21   Willa Cather, p. 421.
22   Patricia McGraw, *Tiffany Blue: The True Story of Turquoise, Tiffany & James P. McNulty in Territorial New Mexico 1892–1933* (Lone Butte Press, 2006), p. 342.
23   Solnit, pp 9–10.
24   Gerald O'Keeffe, *The Ascent of the O'Keeffes: Tracing the First Time the Direct Lineage of Famed American Artist Georgia O'Keeffe to Kanturk, Co. Cork, Ireland* (Original Writing, 2011), p. 192.

REFERENCES

Bloom, Harold, *Anxiety of Influence: A Theory of Poetry* (Oxford University Press, 1997).

Fanning, Charles, *The Irish Voice in America* (University of Kentucky Press, 2000, revised ed.).

McDermott, Alice, *At Weddings and Wakes* (Picador, 2009).

McGraw, Patricia, *Tiffany Blue: The True Story of Turquoise, Tiffany & Co., and James P. McNulty in Territorial New Mexico* (Lone Butte Press, 2006).

ABOUT THE AUTHOR

Eamonn Wall is the author of *Writing the Irish West: Ecologies and Traditions* (Notre Dame, 2011) and *From the Sin-é Café to the Black Hills: Notes on the New Irish* (Wisconsin, 2000), winner of the Michael J. Durkan Prize for excellence in scholarship from ACIS. His poetry collections include *Junction City: New and Selected Poems 1990–2015* (Salmon Poetry, 2015), *Sailing Lake Mareotis* (Salmon, 2011), and *A Tour of Your Country* (Salmon, 2008). With Saeko Yoshikawa, he co-edited *Coleridge and Contemplation* for *POETICA* (Tokyo, 2016), and for Arlen House he edited James Liddy's two collections of literary essays: *On Irish Literature and Identities* and *On American Literature and Diasporas*, both published in 2013. Articles, essays and poems have been published in *The Irish Times*, *The Washington Post*, *TriQuarterly*, *Irish Literary Supplement*, *New Hibernia Review* and other publications. A Co. Wexford native, he emigrated to the US in 1982 and received his Ph.D from the City University of New York-Graduate Center. He lives in St Louis, Missouri, where he is employed as a professor of International Studies and English at the University of Missouri-St Louis where he directs the university's summer study abroad program in Galway and its 'Irish Concerts & Lectures Series'. A past-president of ACIS, he currently serves as a vice-president of Irish American Writers & Artists.

Index

Abiquiu, NM, 5, 187–189, 192–197, 201–202
Aciman, André, 20, 56, 63
African, 189
African American, 154, 160–161
Albany, NY, 67
Albany novels, 22, 174, 181
Albert Hall, London, 155
Albuquerque, NM, 196–197
Alcohol, addiction/alcoholism, 20, 26, 28, 35, 37–38, 44–53, 56, 62–64, 67, 83, 181
Ali, Kazim, 76, 87–8
Allen Randolph, Jody, 130, 137, 145–146
America/n, 9–13, 19–24, 28, 34–36, 38–39, 41, 43–44, 56, 59, 61–64, 68, 70–72, 74–79, 85–86, 88, 92, 95–97, 101, 105–107, 110–111, 113–114, 119–122, 129, 132–134, 136–138, 141–142, 149, 153, 160, 173, 177, 182, 189, 192, 197, 202–204
American Conference for Irish Studies, 13
American Slavery, 154
Annamakerrig, Tyrone Guthrie Centre, 74
Anderson, Nathalie F., 13
Andersson, Claes, 115
Aosdána, 183
Appel, Alfred Jr, 180, 185
Arizona, 191–192
Ars poetica, 143, 169
Art Students League, NY, 190
Atomic Rooster/Vincent Crane, 158

Auden, W.H., 32, 42
Auge, Andrew J., 91, 99, 107–108
Austin, TX, 111, 117

Ballyshannon, Co. Donegal, 151
Bardwell, Leland, 85
Barresi, Dorothy, 87
Bashō, 70
Batten, Guinn, 133–134, 145
Beck, Jeff, 157
Behan, Brendan, *The Quare Fellow*, 44, 77
Belfast, NI, 45, 62, 133–134, 148, 152–155, 157, 163
Bellow, Saul, *Humboldt's Gift*, 40–41, 63
Bernstein, Charles, 41, 117, 119, 122
Berry, Chuck, 152
Berryman, John, *Love & Fame*, 30, 32, 36, 38, 40–1, 61, 72, 114
Bhugra, Dinesh, 52
Bishop, Elizabeth, 31–32, 34, 40–42, 78, 87
Blind Faith/Cream, 155–157
Bloom, Harold, 188, 203
Blues, Delta/Chicago/British, 5, 12, 15, 147–150, 152–154, 156–165
Bluesbreakers, 153
Boland, Eavan, 5, 13–14, 72–74, 84, 88, 125–146, 155, 164, 168, 171–172, 184–185
Bolger, Dermot, 131, 144–145
Bowdoin College, 136

Brautigan, Richard, 113
Brennan, Maeve, 21, 60
Brown, Terence, 27, 61
Brown, Stephanie, 46, 62

Calvino, Italo, 121, 123
Campbell, Neil, 13, 15
Campbell, Siobhán &
   O'Mahony, Nessa, eds *Eavan Boland: Inside History* (Arlen House), 14
Campbell, Wilgar, 157
Captain Beefheart/Don Van Vliet, 154, 158
Cardinal, Ernesto, 106
Carrick-on-Suir, Tipperary, 167, 169–178, 180–183, 185
Carson, Ciaran, *Belfast Confetti*, 168, 180, 184–185
Carthy, Martin, 147
Casey, Philip, 7, 15
Casson, Christine, 13
Cather, Willa, 191, 197, 202–203
Catholic church/Catholicism, 14, 70, 76–78, 84, 91–108, 151, 162, 175, 182, 188, 190, 193
Cerrillos, NM, 187, 198–201
Clancy, Liam, 175, 185
Clapton, Eric, 157
Clark, Heather, 39, 62
Clark, Tom, 115, 122
Clarksdale, Mississippi, 160, 162–163
Clonmel, Tipperary, 170–171
Coady, James & Mary, 173, 175–176, 181–183
Coady, Michael, 5, 13–14, 167–184
All Souls, 14, 167, 168, 170, 172, 174–180, 182–185

Full Tide, 170, 184
Oven Lane, 1, 3, 4, 17, 172, 183, 184, 186
The Well of Spring Water, 174, 185
Cochran, Eddie, 152
Coghe, Jean-Noël, 155, 163–164
Collins, Martha, 77, 81, 88
Collins Press, 163
Coleman, Ornette, 158
Coltrane, John, 158
Connaughton, Marcus, *Rory Gallagher: His Life and Times*, 149–151, 153, 155, 157, 163–164
Conrad Hotel, London, 162
Conrad, Joseph, 21
Cook-Lynn, Elizabeth, 13, 50, 63
Cooke, Barrie, 73–75, 80
Confessional poetry, 20, 28, 31, 35–39, 41, 43, 53–54, 62
Corcoran, Brendan, 62
Corcoran, Neil, 38, 42, 61
Cork, city/county, 60, 147–153, 160, 163, 189, 202–203
Cork Examiner, 147
Cork University Press, 60, 164
Costello, Mary, *Academy Street*, 22–23, 64
Cowan, Robert, 33–34, 61
Crowley's Music Centre, 149–150
Creeley, Robert, 5, 109–123, 141
Cromwell Hospital, London, 147
Cronin, Anthony, *Dead as Doornails*, 44–47, 50, 62
Crotty, Patrick, 27

Cúirt Journal, 73
CUNY Graduate Center, 11
Cyphers, 73

D'Amery, Norman, 152
Daily Mirror, 147
Dardis, Tom, *The Thirsty Muse; Alcohol and the American Writer*, 44, 64
Davis, Francis, *The History of the Blues*, 162, 164
Davis, Miles, 155
Dawe, Gerald, 133, 145–146, 163
De Valera, Eamon, 148
Dean, Joan Fitzpatrick, 13
Deane, Seamus, ed *Field Day Anthology of Irish Writing*, 89
Delanty, Greg, 132, 139
DeLillo, Don, *Underworld*, 23, 64
Dezell, Maureen, 95, 97, 107–108
Diaspora, 20, 57, 65, 69, 85, 135, 138, 141, 167–168, 174–175, 182, 184, 201, 204
Dickinson, Emily, 112
Dickstein, Morris, 11
Dispossession, dispossessed, 160–161, 174, 177, 199
Dixies, 150
Dolan, Joe and the Drifters, 150
Donegan, Lonnie, 152, 156
Doors, The, 155
Dorgan, Theo, 168, 184
Drew, Ronnie, 150
Druid Theatre, 23
Dryden, John, 52, 64
Dublin, Ireland, 4, 10, 23, 26, 28, 30, 32, 42, 44–45, 80, 85, 111, 115, 125–128, 130, 135–139, 149–150, 171, 192
Dublin Opinion, 192
Dubliners, The, 147, 150, 156
Dukes, Carol Muske, 78, 88
DuMars, Susan Miller, 13

Ebest, Ron, 11
Ebest, Sally Barr, 11
Eire-Ireland, 14
Ekenas/Tammisaari, 109–110
Eliot, T.S., 24, 38, 176, 179
Ellington, Duke, 178
Ellison, Ralph, 161
Émigré, 12, 55, 68
Enniscorthy, Co. Wexford, Astor cinema/St Aidan's cathedral, 10, 100, 151
Enniss, Stephen, 27, 29, 35, 45–47, 49–52, 62
Enright, Anne, *The Green Road, The Gathering*, 22–23, 64, 198
Exile, 20, 58–60, 63, 69, 82, 84, 125–128, 130–131, 133, 138–140, 143–145, 161, 167, 175–176, 189

Faber and Faber, 25, 64, 89, 108, 122, 146, 186
Fagley, Katherine, 76, 87
Fairport Convention/Dave Pegg, 158
Fallon, Peter, 73
Famine, Great Irish Potato, 142, 154, 169, 189, 199, 201
Fanning, Charles, *The Irish Voice in America*, 11, 13, 68–70, 73, 85, 87, 140–141, 146, 174, 186–188, 203
Fender Stratocaster, 149, 158
Ferriter, Diarmaid, 148, 163

Fiacc, Padraic, 133–134, 139, 145–146
Finland, 5, 109–111, 115, 118–122
Fitzgerald, F. Scott, 69–70, 135, 162, 192
Fogarty, Anne, 28, 60
Fontana/Impact, The, 152
Ford, Arthur, 113, 123
Friel, Brian, *The Loves of Cass Maguire*, 174, 186
Fulbright, 118–119, 121
Fuller, Blind Boy, 160
Fuller, Louise, *Irish Catholicism since 1950: The Undoing of a Tradition*, 99,101, 108
Furey Brothers and Davey Arthur, 156

Gagarin, Yuri, 192
Gallagher, Donal, 148
Gallagher, Rory, 5, 12, 14, 147–165
Gallagher, Tess, 72
Gallery Press, 25, 60–62, 64, 108, 184–186
Galway, National University of Ireland, James Hardiman Library, 14, 72, 204
Gardiner, David, 14–15
Geldof, Bob, 147
Ghost Ranch, 188, 196, 201–202
Glassman, Dr Joel, 14
Goldhagen, Daniel Jonah, 107–108
Googe, Barnaby, 114
Gordon, Mary, *Final Payments*, 22, 64, 92–94, 96, 107–108
Gorey Arts Centre, Co. Wexford, 15

Grady, Dr Frank, 14
Greeley, Fr Andrew, *The Irish Americans: The Rise to Money and Power*, 95–97, 107
Green, Peter, 156
Greene, Graham, 78
Grennan, Eamon, 35, 61, 63, 72
Guardieff, George, 112
Guibert, Pascale, 13
Gunn, Thom, 113—14, 122
Guralnick, Peter, 161, 164
Gutiérrez, Gustavo, 106

Haavikko, Paavo, 120
Hamill Pete, *A Drinking Life*, 48–49, 64
Hamilton, Ian, *Robert Lowell: A Biography*, 50, 64
Harper, Colin, 152, 155, 158, 163–164
Harvard University, Radcliffe Institute for Advanced Study, Schlesinger Library, 14, 36, 54, 62–63, 72–73, 88
Haughton, Hugh, 27, 29, 34–36, 59–61, 63
Healy, Dermot, 85
Heaney, Seamus, 30, 39, 45, 54, 72–73, 82, 132, 143, 146
Hearn, Patrick, 55
Helsinki, 109–111, 114–121
Hemingway, Ernest, 192
Hendrix, Jimi, 155
Herlihy, Bishop Donal, 100
Hesburgh, Fr Theodore M., 96
Higgins, Kevin, 13
Hinds, Michael, 26, 60
Hodgett, Trevor, 152, 155, 158, 163–164
Holly, Buddy, 132, 152
Homeless/ness, 34, 46

Hooker, John Lee, 160
Horace, 31, 33–34, 43, 61
Hutson, Siobhan, 13
Hynes, Garry, 23

Irish America/n, 1, 3–5, 9, 11–14, 17, 22–24, 48, 55, 64–65, 68–72, 81, 85, 87, 91, 93–94, 96, 102, 107, 123, 125, 128, 135, 138–146, 187–188, 190, 193–195, 198, 201–204
Immigrant, 9, 11–13, 20–21, 28–29, 35, 54–59, 63, 68, 70, 129–130, 137, 140, 181, 189–190, 194, 196, 200
Inwood, NY, 12, 21
Iowa city, 13, 98, 136–137, 143
Iowa, University of, 136, 143
Irish American Writers & Artists, 11, 204
Irish Immigrants in the Land of Canaan, 56–57, 63
Irish Independent, 192
Irish Times, The, 32, 53, 168, 184, 204
Irish Writers Online, 15
Isle of Wight Festival, 155–156

James, Henry, 21
Jamison, Kay Redfield, *Robert Lowell: Setting the River on Fire*, 20, 49–50, 52, 62
Jazz, 157–158, 178–180, 185
Jeffers, Robinson, 141
Jethro Tull, 158
Johnson, Robert, 160–161, 164
Johnston, Dillon, 64, 179, 186
Jones, LeRoi, 154, 164
Joyce, James, 23, 28, 32, 60, 64, 83–84, 89, 103, 148, 168, 170, 178–180, 185–186, 188, 191–192
Dubliners, 23, 64, 89
Ulysses, 103, 168, 178, 179, 185
A Portrait of the Artist as a Young Man, 89, 98

Kandinsky, Vasily, 193
Kavanagh, Fr James, 102, 108
Kavanagh, Patrick, 44, 50, 72, 77, 87, 120–123, 168
Kazin, Alfred, *A Walker in the City*, 29, 64
Kelly, Mary Pat, *Galway Bay*, 11, 22, 64
Kennedy family, JFK and others, 10
Kennedy, Anne, 72
Kennedy, Eddie, 152, 154–155
Kennedy, William, *Ironweed*, 22, 64, 67, 87, 174, 181, 186
Kennedy-Andrews, Elmer, 27, 34, 37, 61
Kenyon, Jane, 82
Kitteringham, Eric, 152, 155
Kilkenny, 74, 85, 180
King's College Hospital, London, 147
Kinsale, 30–31
Kinsella, Thomas, 69, 132
Kirkpatrick, Kathryn, 13
Kirsch, Adam, 35–37, 41, 61–63
Kirwan, Larry, 11
Klein, Michael, 88
Kronborg, Thea, 191, 197

Lake George, NY, 191
Lakota, 50, 98
Lanters, José, 13
Lauer, Robert H., and Jeanette C., 56, 63

Lawrence, Karen, 178–179, 185
Led Zeppelin, 158
Lee, Alvin, 157
Lehman, David, 27, 60
Lendennie, Jessie, 13
Lennon, Prof Joseph, 14
Levertov, Denise, 112, 120, 137, 139
Lewis, Jerry Lee, 156
Lewis, Sinclair, *Babbitt*, 29, 64
Liddy, James, 11, 15, 204
Lloyd, David, 13
Longley, Michael, 39
Lowell, Robert, *Life Studies*, 20, 35–39, 41, 49–50, 52, 54, 62, 64, 72, 78
Lucey, Jim, *The Life Well Lived: Therapeutic Paths to Recovery and Wellbeing*, 20, 51–53, 63
Lynes & Lopez, 202–203

Mac Amhlaigh, Donall, *Dialan Deoraí*, 174, 186
Mac Gabhann, Micí, *Rotha Mór an tSaoil*, 174, 186
MacLeod, Alistair, 129–130, 145
Madec, Mary O'Malley, 13
Madison, James, 101
Maher, Eamon & O'Brien, Eugene, eds *Tracing the Cultural Legacy of Irish Catholicism: From Galway to Cloyne and Beyond* (Manchester University Press), 14
Mahon, Derek, 5, 13, 19–21, 24–62, 64, 139, 172, 186
The Hudson Letter, 24–45, 53–61
New Collected Poems, 25, 26, 61
New Selected Poems, 25, 26, 64

The Yellow Book, 26, 27, 58
Antarctica, 35, 37
Mahony, Christina Hunt, *After the Titanic: A life of Derek Mahon*, 47, 49, 62
Malamud, Bernard, *The Tenants: A Novel*, *The Magic Barrel*, 11, 19, 60
Maritime Hotel, Belfast, 152–153
Masonic Lodge, 200
McAvoy, Gerry, 157, 159
McBrien, Rev Richard, 96–97, 101–102, 108
McCann, Colum, *Let the Great World Spin*, 22–23, 64, 104, 106, 108, 132
McCourt, Frank, *Angela's Ashes*, 22, 102–104, 108, 134, 146
McCracken, Richard 'Charlie', 149, 155
McDermott, Alice, *At Weddings and Wakes*, & *Charming Billy*, 22, 24, 64, 194–195, 203
McDonagh, Martin, *The Beauty Queen of Leenane*, 23, 64
McDonald, Peter, 27, 37, 57, 60
McGahern, John, *Amongst Women*, *The Dark*, 79, 89, 95, 103, 108
McGraw, Patricia, 200, 203
McGreevy, Thomas, 23, 135
McGuckian, Medbh, 45, 83
McKeon, Belinda, 132–133
McNeice, Louis, 40
McNulty, James P., 198–203
Meehan, Paula, 73, 98, 108
Melody Maker, 148

Mental health/illness, 30, 35, 37–38, 48–49, 51–53, 83
Merwin, W.S., 137
Metropolitan Opera House, NY, 178
Milosz, Czeslaw, 69
Milton Academy, 73
Minimalism, 193–194
Missouri, 14, 143, 204
Missouri-St. Louis, Thomas Jefferson Library, 14, 204
Mitchell, Joni, 155
Modernist, 36, 179–180, 185, 188, 193
Momaday, N. Scott, 115
Momaday, Viva Kathleen, 4, 15
Montague, John, *The Dead Kingdom, The Rough Field*, 45, 133–134, 139, 145, 168, 170, 180–181, 186
Montgomery, Little Brother, 160
Moore, Marianne, 135, 141, 146
Morgan, Jack, 11
Muldoon, Paul, *Moy Sand and Gravel*, 22–23, 39, 45, 54, 64, 72–73, 132–133, 139
Munro, Alice, 80
Murphy, Maureen, 11
Murphy, Richard, 191
Murray, Charles Shaar, 154

National Book Award, 73, 81
National Stadium, Dublin, 149
Nationalism, 68, 70
Native American, 98, 199
Nebraska, 15
New Hibernia Review, 14, 62, 184, 204

New Jersey, NJ, 10
New York, 4, 5, 10, 12–13, 19–25, 27–35, 38–43, 45–46, 48, 51–53, 55–61, 63–64, 72–73, 75, 81, 84–85, 108–109, 113, 122, 126, 129–136, 138, 175, 178, 181, 188–191, 194, 198, 201, 204
New York Times, 108–109, 122
New Yorker, The, 136
Newman, Amy, 82, 88
Ni Chuilleanáin, Eiléan, 91
Ní Dhomhnaill, Nuala, 73
Nolan, Janet, 11
Notre Dame, University, 64, 87, 96–97, 123, 146, 202–204

Ó Searcaigh, Cathal, 73
O'Callaghan, Julie, 72
O'Connell, Daniel, 182
O'Connor, Frank, 162, 164
O'Donoghue, Mary, 132, 139
O'Driscoll, Dennis, 73, 81, 85, 88
O'Hara, Frank, *Standing Still and Walking in New York*, 29, 31–32, 64
O'Keeffe, Frank & Ida, 190
O'Keeffe, Georgia, 5, 187–190, 192, 194–197, 200–203
O'Keeffe, Gerald, 202–203
O'Keeffe, Pierce, 189
O'Meara, Timothy, 97
O'Neill, Joseph, *Netherland*, 22, 64
O'Neill, Mike, 200
O'Reilly, Caitriona, 168, 184
O'Reilly, Paul, 13
Oakley, Giles, 160, 164
Olson, Charles, 112, 114, 116, 120

Page, Jimmy, 157
Patton, Charley, 160
Paul, Catherine E., ed *Writing Modern Ireland* (Clemson University Press), 14
Peel, John, *Top Gear/Old Grey Whistle Test*, 154, 159
Perloff, Marjorie, 41
Philadelphia, PA, 13, 175–176, 181–182
Phillips, Robert, 38–39, 41, 62
Plath, Sylvia, 38, 137, 139
Poetry Ireland Review, 60, 73, 174, 184–185
Potts, Donna, 13
Pound, Ezra, 112, 179
Presley, Elvis, 148, 151–152
Princeton University, 54, 185
Punk, 157, 159

Queen's College, New York, 46, 51
Queen's University, Belfast, 155
Quinn, Peter, *Banished Children of Eve*, 22, 64

Raban, Jonathan, 50
Radcliffe College, 73–74, 88
Redmond, John, 27, 29, 42, 60, 62
Redshaw, Thomas Dillon, 14, 145
Reinhardt, Djano, 158
Rich, Adrienne, 43, 137, 139
Ridge, Lola, 141
Robinson, Marilynne, 98
Robinson, Roxana, 188–189, 202
Robinson, Tim, 13, 31
Rockpalast, 159

Roethke, Theodore, 36
Rogers, James Silas, 11, 14
Rolling Stones, The, 156
Rosenthal, M.L., *The Nation*, 20, 35, 61
Royal Showband, 150
Rukeyser, Muriel, 72
Russell, Pakie & Micho, 173–174, 184–185

Saarikoski, Pentti, 111, 115, 122
Said, Edward, 20, 58–59, 63
Salmon Poetry, 74, 204
Sandbrook, Dominic, 126, 145
Santa Fe, NM, 187, 196–197, 199, 201
Schuyler, James, 69
Schwartz, Delmore, 40–41
Scríobh Literary Festival, 85
Sexton, Anne, 38–39, 42–43
Shanley, John Patrick, *Doubt: A Parable*, 23, 64
Sheridan, Jim, *In America*, 22
Shortall, Catherine Mary, 189
Simpson, Eileen, *Poets in Their Youth: A Memoir*, 40–41, 44, 47, 62
Sionnach, An, 14–15
Skinner, Jeffrey, 77, 88
Skinner, Knute, 72
Sligo, Co. Sligo, 13, 72–73, 75, 78, 84–85, 198
Smyth, Gerry, 156–157, 164
Solnit, Rebecca, *A Book of Migrations*, 11–12, 15, 71–73, 86–88, 188, 200–203
Snodgrass, Ann, 38
Spark, Muriel, 20, 64, 78
Spillane, Davy, 156

St Brendan's School, Rathcoole, Mallow, Co Cork, 202
St Louis, University of Washington, 136
Stafford, William, 110, 113–114, 120
Stanford Alcohol Clinic, 46
Stanford University, 132, 135–136, 138
Stein, Gertrude, 94, 112
Stephens, M.G., *Where the Sky Ends: A Memoir of Alcohol & Family*, 48–49, 62
Stevens, Wallace, 23, 59–60, 69, 135, 141, 146, 194–195, 203
Stieglitz, Alfred, 196, 201
Stiff Little Fingers, 156, 159
Substance abuse, 45, 47, 53
Sullivan, Kelly, 27–30, 60
Sun Prairie, Wisconsin, 1, 3, 4, 17, 189–190, 202

Taste, *Taste, Taste on the Boards*, 148–149, 152–156, 158, 165
Tate, Allan, 37, 41
Taylor, Mick, 156–157
Thompson, Richard, 156
Tiffany Company, 198–199, 201, 203
Tillinghast, Richard, 50, 72
Titon, Jeff Todd, 154, 164
Tobin, Daniel, 11, 13, 24, 64, 69–70, 72–73, 85, 87, 119, 123, 139–142, 146, 172, 180, 184–185, 188, 202–203
Irish American Poetry from the Eighteenth Century to the Present, 64, 69, 87
Awake in America: on Irish American Poetry, 87, 146, 188, 202
Tóibín, Colm, *Brooklyn*, 22–23, 65, 71, 104, 106, 108, 128, 130–132, 138, 145
Totto family, 189–190
Trinity College, Dublin, 42
Troubles, the, 133, 159

U2, 147
Undertones, The, 159
Upton, Lee, 82–83, 88
Utah, University of, 136

Valentine, Jean, 5, 13, 67, 69–70, 72–89
Dream Barker and Other Poems, 73–77
Door in the Mountain: New and Collected Poems, 1965–2003, 73, 76, 81, 87, 88
The River at Wolf, 73, 75–78
Growing Darkness, Growing Light, 73–76, 78–80 87
The Cradle of the Real Life, 73, 75, 76, 81, 82, 84
The Under Voice, 74
Van Morrison/Them, 147, 152–155, 163
Vendler, Helen, 113
Villanova University, Falvey Memorial Library, 14
Villanova University, Heimbold Chair of Irish Studies, 14
Vincent, Gene, 152
Virgil, *Georgics*, 82

Wall, Drucilla, 163, 197
Waters, Michael, 76, 87

Waters, Muddy, 156, 160–161, 163
Waugh, Evelyn, 78
Wesleyan University Press, 81, 87, 89
Wexford, 9–10, 23, 42, 99, 129, 150, 172, 202, 204
White, Gillian, *Lyric Shame: The 'Lyric' Subject of Contemporary American Poetry,* 20, 41, 43, 62
Who, The, 155
Williams, William Carlos, 112
Williams, David G., 31, 61
Wilson, John, 149, 155
Wimsatt, William K., 41–42
Wisconsin, WN, 189–191
Wisconsin-Milwaukee, University of, 11, 63, 204
Wittgenstein, Ludwig, 112
Wright, Charles, 137
Wright, James, 137

Yeats, W.B., 32, 75